REVOLUTION AND REBELLION

by
Frank McCulloch

Illustrated by Frank McCulloch, Jr.

SUNSTONE PRESS

SANTA FE

Illustration on page 77 by Carol Snow

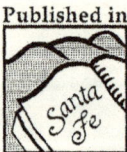

Sunstone books may be purchased for educational, business, or sales promotional use. For information please write: Special Markets Department, Sunstone Press, P.O. Box 2321, Santa Fe, New Mexico 87504-2321.

Library of Congress Cataloging-in-Publication Data:

McCulloch, Frank, b. 1898.
    [Eagle in the sky]
    Revolution and rebellion / by Frank McCulloch; illustrated by Frank McCulloch, Jr.
       p. cm.
    Originally published: Eagle in the sky. c1975. With an additional chapter.
    ISBN: 0-86534-340-3
       1.Pârez, Albino, d. 1837. 2.Governors—New Mexico—Biography.
    3.Mexicans—New Mexico—Biography. 4.New Mexico—History—To 1848.
    5.New Mexico—Politics and government—19th century. 6.Taxation—Political
    aspects—New Mexico—History—19th century. I. Title.

    7800.cbc2 M32 2001
    978.9'03'092—dc21
    [B]   2001049705

Published in SUNSTONE PRESS
Post Office Box 2321
Santa Fe, NM 87504-2321 / USA
(505) 988-4418 / *orders only* (800) 243-5644
FAX (505) 988-1025
www.sunstonepress.com

*Dedicated to my wife
Anna and our children*

TABLE OF CONTENTS

Since REVOLUTION AND REBELLION *is based on numberless stories and anecdotes as told to him by the late Doña Filomena Pérez y Newman de Blanchard Escudero (granddaughter of Don Albino Pérez, the central character in the earlier portions of the book), the author wishes to express his gratitude to her, wishing only that she might have lived to see the book's publication. Dona Filomena's retentive memory and her rare ability to recreate the past were such that she will ever be remembered by those of us who were privileged to know her.*

INTRODUCTION

In the course of any historical research project the researcher eventually reaches that point at which he asks the question, "What is the truth?" After reading ten accounts of the same event and finding as many as seven different sets of "facts," the historian may well wonder if a change of profession is not in order.

This is certainly true in the case of Don Albino Pérez, Mexican governor of New Mexico, 1835-1837. His story is fascinating because he was the first non-native New Mexican appointed to that post after Mexican Independence; he was a rather dashing figure and he was the center of a tragic revolution which ended with his somewhat barbaric death. Though there were no newspapers published in New Mexico during the period, there are contemporary records and one would assume that the facts of Don Albino's life and administration would be easily come by. This, unfortunately, is not the case.

The revolt of 1837 is fairly well documented. Pérez' excessive taxation program was obviously the fuel needed to feed the flames of revolution already ignited by former governor Manuel Armijo and party. José Gonzales' part in the drama is also clear as is that of Diego Esquibel, *alcalde* of Santa Cruz. Scholars seem to agree on causes, dates and battles fought. Pérez, the man, however, remains a mystery. Even the most ordinary events of his life are difficult to trace and historians are at odds over many of them.

One learns, depending on the source one consults, that Pérez brought his wife and infant son with him from Durango. Or, looking elsewhere, one reads that he married Doña Trinidad Trujillo, daughter of a locally prominent family, shortly after arriving in Santa Fe. His son Demetrio was born in the Palace of the Governors in 1836 or 1837. Most sources do agree that Demetrio was born in Santa Fe, but oddly enough, there are no baptismal records of that birth and church records of the period are usually quite complete.

It is generally accepted that Don Albino lost his head after his capture, but three different men are given the dubious honor of having performed the final act. A soldier in the militia is mentioned as having been forced by insurgent Indians to behead his colonel. In other stories it was a Santo Domingo or a Cochiti Indian who did it. The grisly details of the aftermath have been recounted over and over. But the story of how the governor's head was used as a football in an impromptu game at Rosario Cemetery has lately been questioned.

Little Demetrio's fate also has several versions. One is that he was placed outside the city wall by his maternal grandmother on the night of the insurrection; another, that he was hidden in the Church of San Miguel by his great-aunt. Either or both of these acts were performed by his mother. In fact, according to Don Demetrio in his old age, Doña Guadalupe was his maternal grandmother, but his daughter said that Doña Guadalupe was Don Albino's maternal aunt. Thus, even the family does not agree.

The story in this book is drawn from a variety of sources. The political and military parts are based on records and written history. The personal sides of Don Albino's and Don Demetrio's lives are taken from family tradition and the stories handed down by Doña Filomena, Demetrio's daughter. Doña Filomena told the stories she heard from her father. He told the stories he heard from Doña Guadalupe. If the ''facts'' do not always agree with the history books it should be remembered that the history books do not always agree with each other.

Whatever softening of the edges has occurred in the telling is not important. The essence of the man, Don Albino Pérez, emerges. He was a man who dreamed, who tried and who failed. What matters is that he tried.

Wm. Farrington
Santa Fe, New Mexico
August, 1975

CHAPTER I

Durango Is Left Behind

Torrents of rain, blinding flashes of lightning, deafening peals of thunder and an almost continuous darkness combined to terrify the members in one of the strangest *caravanas* ever to travel the tortuous roads of Mexico in 1835.

Many of the individuals in this caravan as it left Durango were aware only of a feeling of regret, regret at leaving their *amigos* and their *primos*, their *bailes* and their *fiestas*, their massive mountain of iron which had seemed to impart to their lives some measure of its own stability. They also missed Durango's magnificent Tuscan Cathedral which their God-fearing ancestors had erected long ago.

Soon, however, abject terror supplanted their feeling of homesickness as the violent storms, unusual for northern Mexico in the spring, continued day after day. But on they traveled, reaching El Coyote and finally the city of Chihuahua. Here the rains suddenly ceased and the sun emerged for the first time in many days, causing this northern Mexican city to assume the aspect of a rose in the desert. It had been cleansed by the rains and now lay resplendent in new sunshine. Even the rugged and barren countryside seemed rejuvenated.

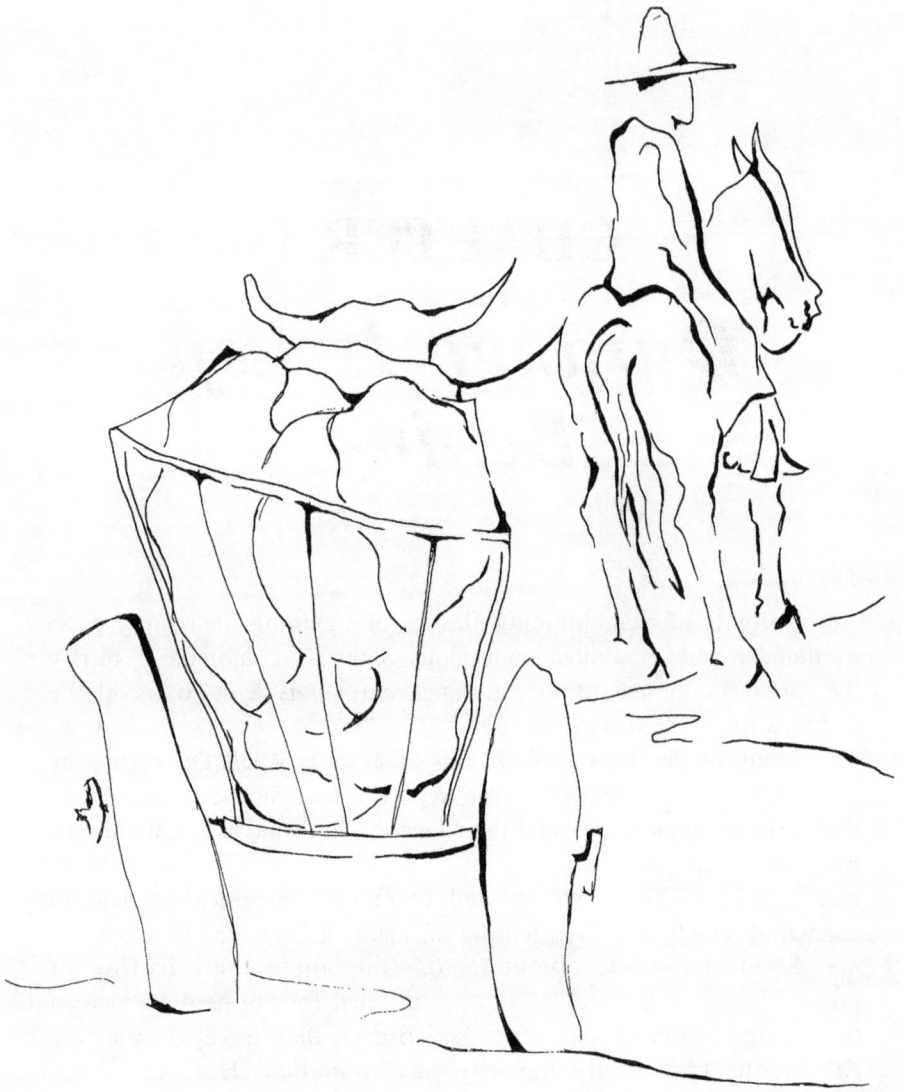

Shouts of joy resounded from those in the caravan because the rains had stopped and because they had once more arrived in the heart of civilization. Never had Chihuahua presented a more welcome sight than it did in the spring of 1835 to this group of travelers, all of whom were a part of the entourage of Colonel Albino Pérez, an officer in the forces of General Antonio López de Santa Ana and now the duly appointed governor and *jefe político* of Mexico's northernmost territory, New Mexico.

Since the countryside was fraught with danger from wild animals and an even more uncertain danger from vengeful Indians, the governor's retinue seemed rather more conspicuous than was prudent. But it must be remembered that no Mexican *hidalgo* would so far forget himself as to travel in an unassuming and unobtrusive manner. Not for Don Albino Pérez to slip quietly into Santa Fe, unheralded and unannounced; rather he preferred to lead an imposing procession which included cavalry officers, lesser members of the Durango militia, three imposing carriages, numerous *carretas* piled high with chests, furniture, trunks and provisions, and sixteen *peones,* leading or riding sixteen burros, bringing up a somewhat desultory rear. Truly, there was something grand about this cavalcade as it moved on and on into the wilderness to the north.

There was nothing grand, however, about the feelings of the lesser members of the Pérez party. Their stop in Chihuahua had been all too brief, and, with the resumption of their journey, they were again filled with nostalgic longings for the simple pleasures which had been theirs in Durango. The *peones* were tempted to flee into the adjacent hills, with a hope of finding some means of transportation back to their beloved homeland. Only a fierce and fervent love for Don Albino, their *patrón,* kept them from carrying out such wild desires, renewed as these desires were every time they passed through some Mexican hamlet where the villagers sat in front of their crude hovels, motionless except for the swaying of their bodies as they sang their native ballads. Don Albino's servants had already seen enough of the world in the monotonous trek from Durango to Chihuahua, and now they wished only that they might go home. Like most Latins, they were at home only where their roots had first been sunk.

As the ornate cavalcade proceeded through the vast stretches of northern Mexico, the Pérez party viewed briefly the Santa Eulalia mines and saw many villages where the inhabitants gasped in wonder at this spectacle of soldiers, civilians, *peones,* blooded horses and patient burros, all a part of the equipment of the newly appointed governor of New Mexico.

First in the line of march were numerous cavalry officers, all a part of Don Albino's command as an officer in the Durango militia. Next came the lesser military personnel, each man on a horse and all forming a combined guard as they rode on either side of the carriages and *carretas* from the front to the rear of the cavalcade. The governor's carriage was next in line, though its sole occupant was a studious individual by the name of Filiberto Saenz whom Don Albino had chosen as his secretary. A learned man and a graduate of the best academy in Durango, Filiberto was not a traveled man and therefore was avidly curious about all he saw. As he rode along, he mused about New Mexico and what he might see in distant Santa Fe and of what his duties might entail as *el secretario* to a colonial *gobernador.* By the side of his carriage, on a magnificent black stallion, rode Don Albino himself. He was too restless to stand the inactivity of sitting quietly in a carriage, and he preferred not to subject himself to the incessant questions which Filiberto asked regarding New Mexico. Don Albino knew little more than Filiberto, and it bothered him no end that he was so poorly informed about the country where he was to be installed as chief executive.

And so, alone with his thoughts, Don Albino pondered whether he would prove to be a wise choice for the position of *jefe político* of a strange and distant province. Of a strong political and military clan, the Pérez family was well known in Veracruz and Durango but would this mean much in distant Santa Fe? Don Albino was not sure. It had been his ardent wish to be a success in his new position, ever since he had heard of his appointment from His Excellency, Don Antonio López de Santa Ana, *El Presidente* of Mexico and the arbiter of the Republic's destiny during much of the time since the break with Spain some fifteen years earlier. As the first governor since the Revolution of 1821 not a native born New Mexican, Don Albino pondered how he would be received in Santa Fe and how he might best serve those who would soon be his responsibility. He had already gleaned some rather discouraging facts — New Mexico was without means; there was practically no system of education, and with the exception of a few *ricos* the people were desperately poor. Here, he thought, were some conditions which he might remedy. Mexico was planning new methods of local government and taxation for its possessions. Don Albino meant to see that through this new scheme of taxation conditions might be improved. With this decision made, the new governor's restlessness subsided and he took on the appearance of a man with a purpose, a man who was making plans.

In the second carriage, regally erect against her velvet cushions, eyes closed against the scenery in which she had no interest, sat Doña Guadalupe Abrigo, Don Albino's aunt and his sole surviving relative. The beads of a rosary slipped through her fingers. A dominant soul, Doña Guadalupe had an air of complete self-satisfaction. She had been praying that the rains would cease, and cease they did. Doña Guadalupe was used to having her own way and she was not particularly surprised that not even heaven would go against her orisons.

Crouched on the floor of the carriage, opposite their mistress, rode her two serving women, Prudencia and Piedad. Being little more than bondswomen and having known nothing all their lives except subjection to the imperious will of the "the last of the Abrigos," one now clutched a chest which contained Doña Guadalupe's jewels while the other held the most cherished possession of her mistress, an intricately carved statue known as *Nuestra Señora de los Remedios*. Doña Guadalupe was proud of her Christian name, of its origin and of the fact that "Our Lady of Guadalupe" had been officially named the Patroness of Mexico. At the same time, however, she turned for divine help to the intercessions of her *Los Remedios*. It was only natural that she should bring the figure along to New Mexico as she had never been separated from it since her father had given it to her years before in Veracruz. Doña Guadalupe was a bit concerned as to what she might find in Santa Fe. She wanted all to go well, and it was her thought that she might bring this about with the help of *Nuestra Señora de los Remedios*.

Old Doña Guadalupe was apprehensive by spells. She was also puzzled and a bit sad that in the evening of her life she should be transplanted to an alien land. In her heart she knew why. Had she ever denied her adored nephew anything? On a day many years ago when Don Albino's mother lay dying she had promised her sister that she would watch over the son being left behind. Doña Guadalupe had kept her word. In fact, she had devoted her entire life to her family and now only Don Albino was left. It was only natural when General Santa Ana suggested that it would be highly appropriate for Santa Fe's Palace of the Governors to have a feminine touch that she should consent to go along. The truth of the matter was that she could not allow Don Albino to go alone into alien surroundings. In Santa Fe her bachelor nephew might find a wife and if this should happen, she certainly intended to have a voice in Don Albino's choice.

El Palacio de los Gobernadores - this sounded good to Doña Guadalupe's ears. She stopped saying her "aves" and dwelt at length on her future as the First Lady of New Mexico, fancying herself as a social leader in the salons of the elect. Resuming her rosary and throwing off worldly thoughts, she glanced at her serving women, and for a moment felt just a bit guilty that she was bringing Prudencia and Piedad into what would amount almost to exile. However, Doña Guadalupe argued with herself, she had never in her life gone out unattended. In Santa Fe, to which she felt she was destined to bring the social graces, even these two personal maids might seem inadequate. Possibly the aunt of a colonial governor should have collected a few more village women as an entourage. However, it was too late now, and Doña Guadalupe was grateful that at least from Prudencia and Piedad she would have no trouble. They would remember that Doña Guadalupe had been a person of prominence in Mexico and that her family had been on terms of intimacy with Emperor Augustín de Iturbide in the brief years of the Mexican Empire. They could be counted on to noise this distinction around the servants' hall of *El Palacio*.

Doña Guadalupe, somewhat inconsistently, chose to forget that when the withdrawal of General Santa Ana's support brought about the end of the Empire and the downfall of Iturbide, the Pérezes and the Abrigos had sided with Santa Ana who had then set himself up as president of the resumed Republic.

CHAPTER II

Across The Frontier

In the third and last carriage, plain and unadorned except for the coat of arms of the Diocese of Durango, rode His Lordship, the Right Reverend José Antonio Laureano de Zubiría, illustrious Bishop of the ancient See of Durango. While reading his breviary with some difficulty because of the deep ruts in the road, he glanced occasionally at his secretary, a tonsured monk from a monastery outside Durango. The monk was busily trying to convince himself that it was the will of God that he should be taking part in this terrifying journey. Thinking longingly of the monastic library where he had been engaged in research regarding the Church in Mexico, Fray Anselmo considered that Bishop Zubiría's diocese was really an ecclesiastical wilderness. He had accompanied the Bishop on one other trip. On that occasion they had gone all the way to Santa Fe. He shuddered when he remembered that journey and was glad that on this visitation they were only going as far as the Rio Bravo del Norte. His Lordship had some diocesan business near El Paso del Norte and it was only to this point that they would be traveling as a part of the Pérez party.

By way of contrast, the good Bishop was sorry that they weren't going to Santa Fe. The Durango prelate had visited Santa Fe only once and that had been two years ago in 1833. However, he

remembered with great satisfaction and joy his reception by the residents of New Mexico's capital city, many of whom had never seen a bishop of their faith. Their enthusiasm had been so spontaneous and unbridled that the good Bishop felt that if he could accompany Don Albino, he might divert some of his welcome to the incoming governor. These thoughts filled the mind of Bishop Zubiría since he knew better than anyone else that Don Albino, a high-born Mexican, would not be welcome in Santa Fe. Don Manuel Armijo would see to that. The Bishop knew the power of Armijo, an ambitious and turbulent demagogue, and he knew that two opposing personalities such as Pérez and Armijo could never be in accord. As the Bishop looked ahead, he was concerned about the possibilities of what might happen. However, he could not help being grateful that an unselfish and philanthropic man was to be at the helm of government in New Mexico, where the poor and the uneducated had received scant attention from Armijo and his kind.

Bishop Zubiría had worried much over the Church in remote New Mexcio, where resident pastors were installed only in Santa Fe, Alburquerque, Taos, Tomé and Santa Cruz. With twenty-six Indian pueblos and many Spanish settlements, the Bishop was hard-pressed for clergy to meet the needs of the Church. Las Vegas, recently founded on the banks of the Rio Gallinas, was already clamoring for a priest. The Bishop of Durango had many worries, and his letters, when not lost at sea, took many months to reach Rome. And now it seemed that along with his ecclesiastical worries, he must concern himself with civic affairs in Santa Fe. The new governor was a friend of his and an ardent son of the Catholic faith. As such, Don Albino could be counted on to do, if humanly possible, the things which the good Bishop had long yearned to see accomplished. Don Albino, a crusader at heart, was a trusting individual and for this reason, Bishop Zubiría was glad that the strong-willed Doña Guadalupe had come along. In many ways, she was a shrewd soul and might be helpful in the uncertain days which lay ahead. She might even be a match for the despot of Santa Fe, Don Manuel Armijo.

And finally came the *carretas* and the burros bringing the supplies and the household goods. Grand as the whole cavalcade was, an atmosphere of gloom pervaded the entire procession and everyone seemed to be filled with a sense of foreboding. Only Don Albino looked ahead with optimism. Plans were shaping in his heart and in his mind. He felt himself to be a deliverer on a sacred mission, a mission which would surely improve the lot of those whom, he already felt, were his people.

On and on went the travelers, day succeeding day, the weeks following one upon another. It was almost too uneventful — ominously so, some of the travelers felt. Finally, after many days of travel, the cavalcade reached a valley immediately south of El Paso del Norte. This was the gateway to New Mexico and for Bishop Zubiría and Fray Anselmo, the end of their journey. Early in the morning the Bishop was saying his last Mass for the members of the Pérez cavalcade. After final prayers were said, and since it was a beautiful spring morning, a festive breakfast table had been set up outdoors for the Bishop, Don Albino, Doña Guadalupe, Fray Anselmo and the ever curious Filiberto, now more excited than ever since New Mexico was actually near at hand, just across the river. The entire group relaxed and were enjoying a last visit, slowly sipping the hot chocolate which was being served by Prudencia and Piedad. Their mistress had brought with her all the necessary paraphernalia for making this delectable drink, so dear to Doña Guadalupe's class. Fate might decree that she should travel through a wilderness but Doña Guadalupe would maintain, as far as possible, the appurtenances of civilization and the niceties of proper living. In her mind, the social graces were just as important on the frontier as in the salons of Mexico City.

In an area close at hand the soldiers' mess had been set up and they, being young and adventuresome, were bemoaning the monotony of their journey and the fact that so far nothing of interest had happened. Not far distant the Pérez *peones* enjoyed a hearty breakfast, preparatory to resuming their journey. To them, also, the trek to the north was becoming more and more tiresome.

Suddenly the horses which were a part of the Pérez party ceased munching their alfalfa and raised their heads in alarm. At the same time the Durango *peones,* ever alert to danger, called out that people were hiding behind the giant mesquite bushes on the hillside. Soon the entire caravan realized that some twenty-five or thirty Apache Indians were encircling the Pérez encampment and closing in from all sides.

Bishop Zubiría, knowing that the missionaries had been able to make very little headway with this particular tribe, besought Almighty God to protect the Pérez party. At the same time he slowly climbed to a spot of ground a little higher than the peaceful breakfast area, where he raised on high the crucifix which he always carried.

20

Absolute quiet reigned as the Bishop, an imposing figure, spoke to the Indians in their own tongue. He paused for a few moments to enable the Apaches to think over what he had said. Then he proceeded.

"My children," said the man of God, "I have spoken to you as the representative of the Christian faith, the faith which teaches that there is but one God, the God of faith, hope and charity. We believe in this one God and we believe that He founded the Church of which I am the Bishop in this vast area. We hope for a life after death, a life which will go on forever. By charity, we mean that we love God and that we love each other. And remember this, we love you, the men of the Apache tribe. You have many gods but you are wrong. I offer you the faith of Jesus Christ. It is mine to offer and yours to accept. I am going to give you my blessing but before I do so, I ask that you cease your molestations of the travelers on the Santa Fe-Chihuahua Trail. When you do this, the one true God will then bless you and yours. And remember, my children, that I am your Bishop also. The Christian religion is not just the white man's faith, it is for all men, all races of mankind."

Then he was silent. To the utter amazement of the Pérez party, most of whom were ready for almost anything, the Indians moved farther and farther away. Seeming to sense the supernatural in what they had heard, they kept their eyes on the silver crucifix which Bishop Zubiría still held aloft. As the Bishop made the Sign of the Cross over these sons of the wilderness and bade them go in peace, the Apaches slowly and silently stole away. The Pérez cavalcade as one man breathed a prayer of relief.

Only the Durango militiamen were disappointed. It had looked for a while as if they might be in for some excitement. But, with a Bishop so closely in league with his Creator, what need had the Pérez party for soldiers at all?

With the dispersement of the Apaches, Don Albino gave the order for departure. He informed his followers that they would now cross the Rio Bravo and that on the other side was New Mexico. Moses, looking into the promised land, was affected no more deeply than was Don Albino Pérez in 1835 when he looked across the river into the land where he was destined to serve as sixty-seventh governor, the ninth under the Mexican regime. The preceding eight had all been native New Mexicans. He was the first Mexican to hold the post.

Bishop Zubiría, sadness written in the lines of his noble face, blessed the entire *caravana* and prayed that their journey to Santa Fe might be accomplished in safety. Don Albino assisted his aunt into her carriage, gave the signal for departure, and the Pérez entourage was on the march again, this time without the ecclesiastical carriage. The good Bishop and Fray Anselmo watched until the cavalcade was out of sight and then sat down to wait. Finally, they heard the shot of a musket and they knew from this signal, previously agreed upon, that the party of New Mexico's governor had crossed the river and was now ready to proceed northward on the soil of New Mexico.

As the caravan arrived on the New Mexico side of the river, Don Albino was seen to kneel and kiss the ground of New Mexico. He gazed steadily to the north and once more gave the signal for departure. They were drawing nearer to Santa Fe, and he had much to do.

CHAPTER III

A Welcome and a Threat

Leaving El Paso del Norte behind, the Pérez party without further mishap wended its way along the Santa Fe-Chihuahua Trail. At least there was no more danger from either the elements or lawless Apache Indians. Even without the Bishop of Durango in person, they knew that his prayers were with them always.

There was some dread in the hearts of the participants as they neared the entry to La Jornada del Muerto, a wild and untamed region about which there were many weird rumors and frightful stories, rumors and stories which grew more weird and more frightening as they were retold by the *peones* in the Pérez party. However, it was a region through which travelers on the Santa Fe-Chihuahua Trail must go, so on they went.

La Jornada del Muerto was situated some sixty miles from El Paso del Norte and extended for another ninety miles to the north. Approximately twenty miles wide, the area was bounded on the east by the San Andres Mountains and on the west by the Fray Cristóbal range. The valley was almost completely arid and covered with heavy sand. The only vegetation was mesquite. The region had served many times as the scene of attacks from Indian warriors, and it was said that one could as easily count the sands of La Jornada as number the lives it had taken. Even the one place where water was available was a natural trap. The Ojo del Muerto, a delightfully refreshing spring, could only be reached by means of a precipitous descent into a narrow canyon, where, since the Ojo was exposed to the view of anyone lurking above, many an unsuspecting traveler had been murdered. Refreshed by spring water, the traveler relaxed and became an easy target for the arrows of Indian raiders.

Don Albino knew that La Jornada del Muerto was an area to be crossed as quickly as possible, and he had no intention of allowing any of his party the doubtful privilege of descending to the Ojo for water. With this in mind he had arranged for the Pérez cavalcade to be amply provided with food and water for man and beast alike.

The dangers from storms, wild animals and savage marauders he left to Doña Guadalupe's *Nuestra Senora de los Remedios,* quieting his own apprehensions with the comforting thought that nothing could happen to a man who had a mission to fulfill. In fact, Don Albino was now quite sure that he was truly "a man of destiny." His followers, now and then fearful of what might lie ahead, needed only to take one look at their leader to be completely reassured. And so, theirs not to reason why, they took their cue from their illustrious *patrón* and at times even resorted to singing the ballads which they had known since childhood. However, they all breathed more easily when they emerged from La Jornada at its northernmost gateway, the village of Val Verde. The village had been abandoned since 1825 when the residents found themselves defenseless against a repetition of Indian raids.

After passing Casa Colorado, the cavalcade spent another two days in Tomé, an important town which had been founded in 1740 as a settlement for redeemed captives, *genizaros.* Belen, with a similar background, also welcomed the governor's party, and here they spent an entire day. In Valencia and Peralta, too, the *caravana* was much made over. The local *alcaldes* made speeches, there was feasting in the daytime and at night a *baile* took place, all of which brought much joy to the members of the Pérez party. These gatherings were enjoyed by Don Albino, since this was his chance to exchange ideas with New Mexicans. He was avid for information about the land where he was to rule as governor, and he would have been less than human if he had not been pleased with the welcome given him and his party. These river towns seemed completely

Perezista in their attitude. In both Tomé and Belen the picture seemed bright.

Nothing is more appealing than the wholehearted welcome of simple people. The residents of all these villages, living as they did close to nature and to the soil of their forefathers, outdid themselves in making Don Albino feel himself a New Mexican. Naturally, he was deeply touched. As for Doña Guadalupe, she had never been so happy in her life as she took to her heart these *rurales* along the Rio Bravo. And Filiberto, he was even more excited than usual as he began to find the answers to many of his questions. Having had only a vague idea about Santa Fe at the beginning of the journey, he was already assembling data and statistics about the capital city, with a few more facts about Taos, Tomé, Alburquerque, the valley of the Rio Bravo and the Rio Arriba country. In fact, Filiberto Saenz was probably the first of a long line of New Mexicans to feel himself an authority on what is today called "New Mexicana."

Everything was going well until the Pérez party, hitherto the recipients of nothing but good news, reached the Plaza de Alburquerque. Alburquerque was a hamlet which had been founded by a handful of Spanish families, several Franciscan friars, and a small garrison of soldiers. Here, the news was not good and Don Albino first learned of the intrigue and dissension already rampant in northern New Mexico. In Santa Fe and Taos there was a growing resentment of General Santa Ana's appointment of a governor who was not a native-born New Mexican. At least this was the reason given and many were impressed by it. They failed to take into account the fact that Don Manuel Armijo, the apparent leader of the anti-*Perezistas,* had once been governor of New Mexico and was extremely ambitious to regain the power he had lost.

Since Alburquerque was Armijo's home town, Don Albino heard quite a bit about Don Manuel during his party's stay in that city. He soon realized that the Armijo forces were to be reckoned with. It was evident on all sides that the former governor and his cohorts were mostly concerned with their own interests and intended to foster these interests through the holding of all the exalted offices in the government of New Mexico. For the present, they were simply biding their time, watching and waiting for this "Veracruz cadet," as the Armijo forces termed Don Albino, to make the first move. Some of this came to Don Albino's ears, and it was indeed disheartening after all the excellent treatment he had received in the southern towns along the river. By instinct, however, he was an optimist and he refused to be upset for long. He was even naive enough to feel that he might win over Don Manuel. The best way to do this, he reasoned, was to retain him in some high office. The newly appointed governor knew that Armijo had frequently been connected with the customs office, and he decided to offer him this appointment again. Maybe this was for the sake of expediency; possibly, it was just good political strategy. At any rate, Don Albino felt that if Armijo was in some office, he might keep quiet. For the present this seemed highly desirable; in fact, it seemed necessary. Don Albino had learned much in Alburquerque.

A Mass of thanksgiving for the accomplishment of their long journey was solemnly celebrated in the one hundred and twenty-five year old Church of San Felipe de Neri, with Don Albino in an honored place in one of the front pews of the church. Following this, the Pérez party moved out of Alburquerque and continued its journey. Bernalillo and Algodones were next on their route and then came the hills, including La Bajada, the ascent of which struck terror to Doña Guadalupe's heart. Prudencia and Piedad were equally frightened, although both of them had by now resigned themselves to almost any fate in this strange and alien land. They felt that they would never see Durango again; if this was the case, they didn't much care whether they lived or died. As their carriage perilously climbed the hills and hurtled down the precipitous descent on the other side, they doubted if they would even live to see Santa Fe. Little did these simple village women realize what they would actually see in the years ahead. Had they known, they would have cared even less about the future.

This journey which had covered so many miles was now drawing to a close, to Don Albino's relief. Bringing so many people on so long a journey was a responsibility, and it would be good to get them all settled.

CHAPTER IV

La Villa Real

Now it was only a matter of hours before the Pérez cavalcade would actually enter the ancient capital of the district of New Mexico — *La Villa Real de la Santa Fe de San Francisco de Assisi.* Don Albino's face brightened as he recognized a group of traders from Chihuahua, their heavily loaded *carretas* slowing their travel to the pace of a snail. The traders made way for the Pérez party to go around them, and Don Albino waved them his appreciation. In his efforts to glean information about New Mexico, he had learned that these traders and their wares represented a great advantage for both Mexico and New Mexico. This overland commerce had mounted from fifteen thousand *pesos* in 1822 to around a half million *pesos* in the year which preceded his arrival in New Mexico.

Reaching the Agua Fría section of Santa Fe, Don Albino brought to a stop his faithful Prieto, a coal-black stallion, and waited for all of the members of his party to assemble. Any sort of formation in the *caravana* had been lost in the many miles of endless travel. Now that they had reached their goal, he felt that some degree of order should be restored to give the processional the necessary dignity which Santa Feans would surely expect from one who was coming to them as a ruler.

The party was ready to proceed when it was held up again. Numerous residents of Santa Fe, having heard the news of the governor's arrival, pressed in from all sides. There were cries of welcome as they glimpsed Don Albino Pérez on his ebony-hued mount. The spectators even forgot that such a demonstration might bring dire reprisals when brought to the attention of the despotic Armijo, whose spies were on hand to see the entry. The air resounded with shouts of "Viva El Gobernador." *Los trovadores,* from the plaza, soon formed themselves into a makeshift band, and all was in readiness for the short march still ahead. To the strains of *Blanca Flor,* played by the hurriedly assembled musicians, Don Albino made his triumphal entry into *La Villa Real* as the duly appointed *jefe político* of New Mexico and the properly accredited emissary of Don Antonio López de Santa Ana, *El Presidente,* dictator and strong man of Mexico. The Durango militia was somewhat bedraggled and the *peones* were dejected and skeptical, but the new governor was a magnificent figure and quite sure of himself as he guided his horse through the streets of Santa Fe, smiling to the right and to the left.

The fears which had been in Don Albino's heart during his short stop in Alburquerque were gone. As the Pérez entourage neared the ancient Palace of the Governors, he felt himself to be another crusading Oñate or a conquering De Vargas. Dismounting, he turned to flash an engaging smile at Doña Guadalupe, now almost overcome with joy as she shared in this big moment in her nephew's life. She had finally convinced herself that she, too, was playing a role in the destiny of New Mexico and that she had actually reared Don Albino for this auspicious occasion. True, she had experienced a moment of disappointment when she first saw the Palace of the Governors on the north side of the city's plaza. She had expected a modified reproduction of Chapultepec, at least. However, the moment was fleeting for she felt that she was walking across the pages of history, history yet to be made.

Her spirits at any rate were not going to be dampened by the fact that the Palace of the Governors had dirt floors. She had great respect for things which were old and venerable, durable and lasting, and when Filiberto told her that the building was already over two hundred years old, she looked at it with increased respect mingled with awe. Filiberto's avid curiosity for statistics and information did serve a purpose.

As the governor and his small retinue waited for the welcoming committee to appear, the band continued with *Blanca Flor,* the one tune they all seemed to know. Shortly, several New Mexicans, resplendent with plumes and medals, came forward with outstretched hands and ingratiating smiles. And their leader was, of all people, Don Manuel Armijo, one-time governor of New Mexico and still an aspirant for the position of chief executive, and also presumably the undercover leader of the anti-*Perezistas.* Taken aback for a moment, Governor Pérez acknowledged the highly embellished words of welcome which came from the lips of Don Manuel. He was introduced to the Armijo cohorts and in turn presented the committee to Doña Guadalupe and the more important members of his entourage.

The flags of the Mexican Republic flew over the Palace of the Governors and in the plaza. When Don Albino saw the Eagle of Mexico, he felt reassured. With this emblem floating against the blue skies of Santa Fe, it was impossible to feel himself a stranger. And he needed this reassurance. He felt, or did he imagine it, that with the appearance of the powerful Armijo, the cries of "Viva El Gobernador" had become less enthusiastic. The brilliance of the occasion seemed somewhat clouded, and a vague uneasiness fluttered about the edges of his mind. It was not strong enough to be called a premonition, and yet the governor felt a sudden chill.

It was too late for turning back. The stage was set and Don Albino's die cast. An idealist, he wanted only to help his people, and most of them wanted no help from him. As the two opposing factions, each outdoing the other in Latin politeness, entered the Palace of the Governors and the heavily carved doors closed behind them with an ominous thud, "Viva El Gobernador" was heard no more.

A hush had fallen on the plaza.

CHAPTER V

A Meeting of the Council

Many months passed. That April day in 1835 when Don Albino's cavalcade had entered Santa Fe, its leader filled with high hopes for the welfare of his people, was only a faint memory. It was now 1837 and another meeting, one of many, was drawing to a close in the executive offices of the Palace of the Governors. To Don Albino, these meetings seemed the worst of all his tribulations, for they were filled with endless conversations composed of empty words.

Blocked at every turn, misunderstood by one group and mistrusted by another, the Governor of New Mexico was trying to ward off a feeling of utter disillusionment as he prepared to close today's meeting with an important announcement to his unofficial cabinet. These were the men to whom he looked for advice and counsel. Don Albino had chosen these men soon after his arrival in Santa Fe. He had chosen them because of their knowledge of New Mexico, but he knew that knowledge was not enough. His choice had been hasty because of his desire to serve the people but he realized now that he was not sure of some of the men. At least one of them had no liking at all for the Pérez administration.

However, Don Albino also knew the folly of surrounding himself with men who always saw eye-to-eye with him. Refusing to recognize the fact that a definite line was drawn — that Santa Fe was made up of *Perezistas* and anti-*Perezistas* — the governor preferred to think that the *políticos* of the capital city were either in sympathy with his plans or, for sincere and good reasons of their own, not yet able to go along with him. Life is often difficult for those individuals who can see both sides of a question, and such a man was New Mexico's governor in 1837. An almost naive statesman of high purposes and ideals, Don Albino found Santa Fe's political structure hopelessly involved.

Seated at the head of a massive and highly polished table, surrounded by his cabinet, Governor Pérez looked weary. His deeply lined face reflected the strain of the worry and uncertainty which had been his lot since he arrived in Santa Fe. Despite the fact that he did have a few loyal and stalwart supporters, he realized with bitterness that some of his associates were incapable of telling the truth. Their only reason for attending these meetings was to keep the opposition informed as to what went on in the Pérez administration and in the mind of Don Albino Pérez. However, Don Albino had won some of the arguments today, and, tired though he was, he was aware of a certain triumph. He knew that his program of taxation, with the full approval of Mexico, would soon be put into operation. Much as he disliked imposing taxes on *los pobres,* many of whom seldom saw more than a *peso* or two at one time, the governor envisioned tax money converted into schools. From these schools would come generations of educated New Mexicans assuring better days for New Mexico.

As he was about to begin his prepared discourse, Don Albino heard a sound that caused him to stop. The soft tones of a lullaby came from an adjoining room. He knew that near one of the corner fireplaces sat his wife of less than two years and Doña Guadalupe. In the room seated on a hassock, was Doña Guadalupe's former serving woman, Prudencia, now transformed into a nursemaid. She was holding in her arms the son of the governor, one month old Demetrio. His old smile, seen so often in the days in Durango but rarely evident in recent months, lighted Don Albino's face as he thought of his family.

He had married shortly after his arrival in Santa Fe and leaned heavily on his newfound domestic happiness. This happiness had enabled the governor to continue his righteous crusade in behalf of honest government and his noble efforts for the poor and the unfortunate. Not long after arriving in Santa Fe, Don Albino had met the Trujillo family and had fallen in love with their daughter, Trinidad. Like many men who have remained single until near middle age, he had conducted his courtship in an impetuous manner which had completely swept the sheltered young Trinidad off her feet. The Trujillo family, truly of the *gente fina,* permitted all this because they, too, were carried away with the charm and breeding of this high-born Mexican. They gave their consent to the early wedding that took place in the *Parroquia* of St. Francis. They were married by the Very Reverend Juan Felipe Ortiz, the representative of the Bishop of Durango in New Mexico. This member of the clergy was the *Vicario* of Santa Fe and was to figure prominently in the affairs of the Pérez family as long as he lived.

Since Don Albino's bride was the granddaughter of Don Bartolome Fernández, a Captain in the Spanish army in the early 1700's, whose gallant defense of his king had won him a grant of some 2,500 acres of land near Santa Fe, it was inevitable that Doña Guadalupe should welcome her nephew's bride to the Palace. She delighted in showing *La Señora del Gobernador* the endless rooms of the venerable building, as well as the silverware and gold plate, the laces and velvets, the linens and the ornately carved furniture, all of which had been brought from Mexico in the Pérez *caravana.* Within a year, the bells of the churches in Santa Fe had announced the birth of little Demetrio. It was then that Doña Guadalupe knew her greatest happiness. It far offset any feelings of reluctance which might have been hers when she was called upon to relinquish her prerogatives as the first lady of New Mexico. The same feeling of possessiveness which she had felt for Don Albino was being repeated as she held his infant son in her arms. In fact, she could hardly wait for the time when Doña Trinidad would resume her place by her husband's side in the social life of Santa Fe. When this was accomplished, *Tia* Guadalupe would see to it that she herself was in complete charge of the Palace nursery, where she could direct Prudencia in the care of the infant Demetrio, for whom nothing was too good.

Literally forcing himself to discontinue the pleasant contemplation of his family, Don Albino looked around the table. Without preamble the governor started to speak to his cabinet. "Gentlemen, before we discuss the business which must be accomplished today, I must inform you that I have had a letter from the former governor of New Mexico, Don Manuel Armijo, written from his home in Alburquerque.''

The first to find his voice among the group of startled and wary advisors was Don Jesús María Alarid, Departmental Secretary. "What can he want? If Don Manuel has written you a letter, he has a reason for so doing. He also has something on his mind, or more properly, something up his sleeve.''

"Let me tell you its contents, my friends,'' said Governor Pérez. "There is no point in reading the letter to you, as both Filiberto and I have found it completely meaningless. We have tried to read between the lines but for the life of me, I can't see why he chose to write. He assures me of his undying devotion to me and to my administration. He regrets that I listen to talebearers and false friends. He also feels that it is unfortunate that I have taken cognizance of his troubles with the *Tejano,* Señor Fox. He then loses himself in an attempted explanation of the numerous loans he has received from Señor Fox and many others. It all boils down to a feeble excuse for the graft and thievery which has been the curse of the customs office. I am now inclined to think that it is a good thing Don Manuel is no longer an official there.''

Don Santiago Abreu, a former *jefe político* and an ardent supporter of the Pérez administration, replied to the governor's words. "I am sure that we all agree that the customs office is a better place without the services of Don Manuel Armijo. Personally, I would like to see him exiled to Chihuahua. At least, we might keep him out of Santa Fe.''

"We all know that Don Manuel hatches plots and schemes while he is in Alburquerque and that on his frequent visits to Tomé he incites the people there to dissatisfaction and restlessness,'' said Governor Pérez, now almost ready and willing to suspect his predecessor in office. "I respect your judgment, Don Santiago, but I cannot agree with you that it would be wise to keep Don Manuel out of Santa Fe. I feel that we are much safer from his intrigues if he comes and goes under our eyes. He has many friends here in Santa Fe and if he is refused entrance, we will only further alienate his supporters.''

Don Jesús María Alarid rose to his feet and for the second time addressed the group. As the departmental *secretario,* he had a good concept of the danger which might come from Armijo's plots. "*Mi Gobernador,* every time Don Manuel comes to Santa Fe he does further harm to our cause. He tells the lowliest of our *peones* that they will be taxed unmercifully when our program goes through. He tells them that while their families languish and die with the smallpox, the Pérez family lives in a luxury hitherto unknown in Santa Fe. He even has them looking through the windows of the palace and, of course, the hungry *peones* are impressed. They do not know that all these furnishings and paintings were brought by you when you came from Mexico.''

After pausing for breath, the departmental secretary continued, ''And the *ricos,* they've all been told that they will lose their fortunes through taxation and that under your system of education, all the sheepherders must go to school. They will be brought in from the Rio Arriba and the Rio Abajo, from the Taos Mountains, from the Rio Gallinas valley and from the hills which border La Jornada, all to be enrolled in schools, and who will watch over the sheep? He hates you, Don Albino, and there is nothing you can do which will be acceptable to Don Manuel and his gang of robbers, all of whom fear him more than they do you. He wants again to be the governor and now that you have removed him from the lesser office which he discredited so shamefully, his bitterness has increased. He has ridden roughshod over his friends and his enemies and has achieved a position of power through the fear which he has aroused in the hearts of many of our people. When he was in favor with General Santa Ana, all was fine. Now that you have supplanted him he hates you and calls you the 'aristocratic stranger.' He hates all of us who are a part of the Pérez administration, but, most of all, he hates those whom he labels *los gringos,* though he is not above dealing with them, accepting their bribes and promising them favors if he is returned to power.''

Alarid had scarcely finished when a dark, pock-marked man who had remained strangely silent until now, flared out, ''And why shouldn't we all hate these *gringo* devils? They laugh at our way of life but drive hard bargains when their *carretas* roll into the plaza. They double the price when they see our people, selling them a lot of useless things for which they have no need. As surely as my name is Gomecindo Bustamente, I say 'Death to these *gringo* swindlers.' ''

CHAPTER VI
"The Alcalde From The River"

The oldest man in the room, Don Juan Cristóbal Vigil, felt that it was high time his voice was heard. He rose to his feet and in the soft and dulcet accents of his Andalusian ancestors, spoke to the gathering, "It is a mistake for us in New Mexico to resent those from the States. As long as we feel this way, we will have trouble and bloodshed. No one race of mankind is filled with virtue and no one nationality is free from vice. Can we not learn to evaluate our fellow men as individuals? You all know that for many years I was the *alcalde* over near the river. In those years, I met all sorts of men. I have dealt with *los americanos,* good ones and bad ones. They differ very little from any other nationality." With these words the old judge sat down.

But the swarthy Bustamante, already filled with chagrin because he had revealed his anti-*Perezista* leanings, plunged into an angry and uncontrolled tirade, "We all know, Don Cristóbal, of your fondness for *los americanos,* as you prefer to call them. We also know that not only in your court were you associated with them. Important men from Washington were in your home only last week. And you sit in the plaza for hours with that *rico* from New

York, the consumptive one. It is a common sight to see you and the 'mountain men' together; they go and come to your house by the river. These 'mountain men' are infesting our hunting grounds; they fish in our rivers, and they grow rich when they sell their buffalo pelts here in the Santa Fe market.. And if you deny my accusations, then why did you learn the English language? Answer me these questions, Don Cristóbal.''

None of this explosive monologue seemed to affect the patience of Don Cristóbal Vigil. Without raising his voice, he turned to Bustamante, now almost beside himself with wrath, and said, ''My friend, your anger will consume you if you don't control it. I wish that I did not have to dignify your accusations with answers but I will give you the courtesy which you have failed to give this august assembly. Yes, my friend, I have entertained many Americans in my home, men whom you scornfully refer to as *los gringos*. And it is well for New Mexico that I have done so. Through them I have learned that in the city of Washington even President Andrew Jackson is alarmed at some of the things which go on here in New Mexico. Too many *americanos* have had trouble in our fair land, too many for the government in Washington to ignore. Eventually, our difficulties must be settled, and this may mean war. It will surely mean war if you, Señor Bustamante, and your kind remain adamant against everything which comes from outside.

''Furthermore,'' continued the wise old sage from the river, ''I have learned many things from the *americanos* which have nothing to do with our political strife, things which might put our poor land to shame. Did you know that in New York City newspapers are sold on the streets for one *centavo?* Even the poor people buy these newspapers and read them. Can you imagine? Poor people read. And they not only read. Many of them can write fluently, not just their names. Might it not be well if such a condition existed here in Santa Fe?

''I am glad to see my friends, the three Abreu brothers, here today. They share my views on literacy. As you know, they brought the first printing press to New Mexico and published *El Crepúsculo* in Taos. I hope that they may soon resume publication and that we may have a similar journal here in Santa Fe. But what good will newspapers do our people unless they learn to read?''

Old Don Cristóbal paused for a moment and considered before continuing. ''You mentioned also my friendship for the 'mountain men', Señor Bustamente. They have been in my home, yes, though

38

I must admit that they have not sat at my table. The women of my family would scarcely countenance the manners of these men from the United States. But as far as their hunting and fishing go, aren't there enough buffalo, deer, wild foul and fish in this vast land for all? As for my speaking the English language, I thank you, Señor Bustamante. I dare say that my linguistic abilities would harldy be noteworthy in regions where the English language is spoken. I have been fortunate in having advantages not usually given to New Mexicans, and I did learn something of the English language when I was in school in Mexico. Therefore, it does give me pleasure to speak this language when I get a chance.

"But let me finish, I have taxed the patience of this assembly enough. I am an old man, and to old men is sometimes given the gift of vision. As I look into the years ahead, I can see hundreds, nay, thousands, of men and women crossing these mountains from the East, bringing with them new customs and new manners of living from their homes in the States. When that day comes, I pray that they, *los anglos,* may live in peace with Spaniard, Mexican and Indian alike. I was born here in Santa Fe during the years when the ancestors of these *americanos* were fighting for freedom from England. That was long ago, and I was proud to be called a Spaniard then. When I had already reached mature years, we freed ourselves from our own mother country, and now that the Eagle of Mexico flies over this venerable building, we are proud to call ourselves Mexicans. If we here in New Mexico do not take care of our affairs properly, then it may be that *los americanos* will come, not to merge themselves and their customs with the traditions which are ours but as conquerors. I am nearing the end of a long life and I believe that it has been a useful one. I may not live to see many more changes. Soon I shall be gathered to my fathers but I trust that my children and my children's children will witness the days of enlightenment which are a part of your plans, *mi Gobernador.* Your Excellency, a thousand pardons for the time I have taken. You have been truly kind to an old man who has grown loquacious with the years. I thank you." With these words, old Don Cristóbal Vigil, worn out by his own oratory, sat down, whispering to himself, "Por Dios y mi Patria."

Silence ensued for a few moments as the advisors of the Pérez administration recovered from Don Cristóbal's dramatic discourse. Then the silence was broken by the departmental secretary, Don Jesús María Alarid, "My felicitations, Don Cristóbal. We all know the part you have played in the life of Santa Fe and I wish that we had more men of your stamina and courage. But *los americanos* are not coming today and when they do, I, for one, have little fear that they will come as conquerors. It is the present of New Mexico with which we must deal now. Our governor has taken care of this need and we are eager to know the details of his plan. Let us give our attention to His Excellency." Turning to the governor, he said, "Don Albino, we are at your service."

CHAPTER VII

"Taxes For New Mexico"

Governor Pérez rose to his feet and looked into the eyes of every man gathered around the council table, "Gentlemen, when I had been in your country, now my country, but sixty days, I spoke from the *portal* of this building. I told the populace in the plaza that I, their new governor, felt that the people of New Mexico were men and women who loved law and order and were naturally obedient and cooperative. I sensed that they were fundamentally peaceful citizens and that, as a people, they were in favor of justice. In the practice of their civic and moral virtues, I believed that they wished to lead peaceful and quiet lives as God intended and for which the people of this area were particularly fitted.

"I have now been in New Mexico for two years," he continued. "It is my pleasure to renew these statements made in the spring of 1835. I know New Mexicans better now, and I also know the conditions here. I feel that our chief need is education. The youth of Santa Fe and of all the other towns in the province, and this includes the villages in the mountains, must learn to read and write. It may be some years before newspapers are sold and read in this city, but the day will come when journals will be printed in Santa Fe. I am happy to prepare for that great day. But first, we must have education for all. You have heard me say this many times. Now, my friends, we have the means to provide this schooling and it gives me extreme pleasure to say that my *pronunciamento* will be posted in the plaza within a few days."

Don Albino looked almost young again as he warmed to his subject. The men who were gathered around the council table listened eagerly. The governor continued, "Our plan for taxation is well known to all of you but now that we have the sanction and approval of Mexico, it is my desire to review the details of these taxes. In Santa Fe and in all of the towns of New Mexico there will be a tax of two dollars for each theatrical performance. The same amount will be levied against each owner of a vehicle used for the hauling of merchandise. Two dollars will be charged for each merchant who sets up a store, and without this license he cannot operate his business. For each horse or mule sold, a tax of two dollars will be deducted from the selling price. Permits for a dance will cost fifty cents. Each man who cuts timber will be required to obtain a permit which will cost five dollars. A charge of twenty-five cents will be made for each animal which is allowed to roam freely through the streets of our cities. A like amount will be assessed against the owners of horses and mules when these animals are used to haul wagons for commercial purposes.

"You have heard the figures which we have agreed upon," he continued, "and I ask that you also listen to some regulations which will be a part of this tax program. All strangers with no visible means of support will be arrested by the local *alcaldes*. They will be punished and required to obtain employment. Justices of the Peace, all over the district, will be required to enforce these regulations. Failing to do so, they will lose their official standing, they will be fined the sum of five dollars and they will incur the censure of their fellow citizens."

The governor waited again for a few moments and then proceeded. "I know, my friends, the hardships which these taxes will cause many of our people in the beginning. But from time immemorial, progress has come through taxation. The great San Mateo, chosen by our Lord as one of His own, was a tax collector, so you can see that what we propose today is really nothing new. You all know that the revenues from the customs offices have been negligible and that the graft in those offices has been deplorable.

What we propose now is taxation in a more equitable manner. I already have honest men to make the collections and in the disbursements for eduction and relief, you yourselves, gentlemen, will have a voice. Meanwhile, I solicit your support in helping our people understand that this method of taxation is the best way, the only way. If you can convince the people of Santa Fe that we are right, all of New Mexico will follow. Once this is done, the rest will be easy. Through these expected revenues, we will eventually have educated New Mexicans and happier New Mexicans.''

Don Albino's listeners were enthralled by the governor's ardent discourse and by the sincerity behind it. "Viva El Gobernador," shouted the members of the cabinet on that memorable day as the meeting came to a close. Perhaps he was a dreamer of dreams, but now, they were going to see some action.

Noticing that Don Albino was waiting for their renewed attention, the advisors stopped to listen once more. "Come, my friends, we will now pay our respects to the ladies of my family. I am sure that they will have prepared for your visit with some of my aunt's spiced brandy and *bizcochitos*. It will also give me much pleasure to show you my son, Demetrio. I feel that our actions of this morning have assured his future and the future of all of the children of New Mexico. Unlimited opportunities will be theirs. Proceed, gentlemen. Our cares are over for today. Tomorrow will come, yes, but now we will drink to my little Demetrio and to future New Mexicans, that they may be allowed to welcome the dawn of a better day.''

As the governor and his friends entered the *sala* where the Pérez family was gathered, the pock-marked man from Alburquerque was seen to slip through a side door of the Palace. He hurried across the plaza and down the narrow streets to the Alameda where Don Manuel Armijo impatiently awaited his report.

CHAPTER VIII

Revolution and Rebellion

Never was a New Mexican spring so beautiful as it was in 1837 and never was it so thoroughly ignored by the inhabitants. Little was heard about the planting of corn, chili and beans, a topic which usually occupied the thoughts of all New Mexicans and resulted in endless discussions in the *placitas* of every town and village. Now the talk was devoted exclusively to the possibility of civil war. Rebellion and revolution seemed inevitable as the chasm between the *Perezistas* and anti-*Perezistas* widened. The *ricos* were divided, and the *peones* were divided. The military forces did not agree, and the various Indian tribes, seldom in accord, were less united than ever. New Mexico was truly a seething cauldron of agitation, hate, suspicion and intrigue. And all this unrest was ignored in Mexico, too far away and too busy with its own political troubles to bother about the isolated department to the north.

Don Albino's tax program had been introduced, and he had left nothing undone to see that a rigid enforcement was accomplished and the revenues disbursed properly. Naturally, this did not endear him to the men who had been used to handling government funds.

A certain portion of the collections had always been sent to Santa Fe where it all legitimately belonged, a part had gone to numerous "middle men" and, of course, the agents had never failed to line their own pockets thoroughly. Now that they were *persona non grata* in the Pérez administration, there was only one thing for these frustrated renegades to do, and they did it. They went over to the other side and thus augmented the already growing ranks of the anti-*Perezistas*.

Authorities do not agree on precisely what brought about the revolution of 1837. It is most probable that it grew and eventually exploded for a number of reasons. In an area so vast that its boundaries were neither defined nor recorded, each reason seemed small and unimportant, but all combined to bring about one thing: hatred of Governor Albino Pérez.

Soon after Don Albino's arrival in New Mexico, he had been called upon to settle a dispute in Santa Cruz, where Diego Esquibel was the *alcalde*. Several residents of Santa Cruz had brought a suit against some of their neighbors because of unpaid debts. The defendants were all related to Esquibel, and the *alcalde*, being convinced that blood is thicker than water, simply decided the case in favor of his *primos* and closed the arguments. Later, when the decision was reversed in Santa Fe, Don Albino removed Esquibel from office, thus alienating half the village of Santa Cruz, which in those years was one of the political centers of New Mexico.

A similar situation arose in New Mexico's Department of Customs where the top officials had been evicted and replaced by that intrepid office holder, Don Manuel Armijo. Upon learning that the original officials had been wronged, Governor Pérez reinstated them and ousted Don Manuel. The Armijo influence was great, and the repercussions were, therefore, louder and longer than in the Santa Cruz affair. The Esquibel relatives were many but Don Manuel Armijo was the most influential man in all of New Mexico and those who opposed him walked on dangerous ground.

Another source of trouble plagued the governor at this time. When Mexico had freed herself from Spain and changed her name from New Spain to Mexico, she wanted nothing more to do with Spain and Spaniards. Therefore, the Expulsion Laws were passed stating that all Spaniards must leave Mexico and Mexican colonies. Just what constituted a Spaniard had never been very well defined, and Santa Fe, taking the easiest path, simply ignored the regulation. It might have been better had Don Albino followed the same course, but he didn't. If a law was in effect, he reasoned, it should be enforced. Therefore, the Spaniards would have to go. The governor decided that this included everyone who had been born in Spain. Unfortunately, some of the clergy were natives of Spain but had no wish to abandon their posts in the new world. A devout son of the Church and devoted to the faith of his fathers, Don Albino now found himself in trouble with the Spanish clergy.

Certainly, New Mexico was not a place of peace and harmony. Because of all the troubles which beset the district, it was not difficult for the leaders of the various factions to band together under the guise of a "no taxation" platform. The next step was to rid Santa Fe of the Pérez regime once and for all. And who better to carry out a revolution than the Indians, always ready for a chance to retaliate against those who had taken their lands. Just who was able to convince the northern New Mexico Indian tribes that Don Albino Pérez was the symbol of their enemies will never be known. It is clouded in mystery, and succeeding generations of historians have failed to uncover the strategy which brought this about. Don Manuel, of course, was always a logical suspect, but nothing could be directly attributed to him. All indications still point in that direction, however.

By the time summer arrived, the anti-*Perezistas* in their headquarters in Santa Cruz were joined by Indians from Taos, San Juan, San Ildefonso, Santa Clara, Nambé and Cuyamungue. They elected José Gonzales, an Indian of mixed ancestry from Taos, as their leader. They then drew up a plan with the high-sounding name of a "Declaration of Principles." This was a dramatic document which refused Mexico's plan for departmental government of her colonies and also refused the acceptance of any sort of taxation. They vowed that for their "Principles" they would gladly shed their blood to the last drop. The declaration was purported to be the brain child of José Gonzales, which is highly unlikely. Until the excitement began in Santa Cruz he had been quite happy to be a buffalo hunter and it is doubtful that he was even literate.

The document was dated August the Third, 1837.

And so, while double-dealing hands remained concealed, Indians from all over northern New Mexico made their plans, plans which called for the capture of the governor and the seizure and subjugation of Santa Fe. The second part of the plan originated in the minds of the Indians themselves, and this greatly alarmed the unknown leaders as they saw the revolution getting out of hand.

They wanted very much to eliminate Don Albino Pérez but they had certainly not counted on their capital city falling under Indian domination. They all knew too well the stories of 1680 when the Pueblo Indians had banded together and taken Santa Fe. The Mexican leaders did not relish a repetition of that revolt.

That this uprising was not fostered by Indians alone was shown clearly by a popular poem of 1837. It was recited or sung all over the territory and started with these words:

> *Mexicanos Cañaderos*
> *Camisa de balleton*
> *Que dejaron sus familias*
> *Por sequir la revolución.*

> Mexicans from La Cañada
> With shirts of home-spun yarn
> Who left their homes and families
> To follow the revolution.

On they came, disgruntled Mexicans and Indians, a motley of ruffians and insurgents, many of whom had been peaceful farmers and contented *viñeros* until now. All at once, however, they had been transformed into a bloodthirsty mob. It was a dangerous crowd of malcontents which emerged from the plaza of Santa Cruz. Indians, yes, but it was a rare sight to see, here and there, a *Mexicano Cañadero*.

Events related to political intrigue are seldom kept very confidential; before long, all this was heard in the offices of the Palace. Don Albino saw that the time was past for merely posting rules in the plaza. The rebellion must be put down once and for all. The governor sent riders in all directions, requesting volunteers to hasten to Santa Fe and join in the march on the insurgents to the north. These recruits were merged with the Santa Fe militia, and from the activities in the plaza, it was evident that New Mexico was preparing for war. The military force of New Mexico was comprised of approximately two hundred men. This was the best that the Pérez administration could do.

In the midst of all these preparations, the governor of New Mexico was busy at his desk. He was hurriedly taking care of last-minute but vital matters. There he was joined by his supporters, all ready to follow their leader into battle.

"Gentlemen," said Don Albino, resplendent in his Colonel's uniform and a long, enveloping cloak, "We have little idea of what we face. Our forces are not large, as you well know, and we have no idea of the numbers of *revolucionarios* who are scheduled to leave Santa Cruz today. We are informed that their plans call for the seizure of Santa Fe and the taking of this building. I know that you share my hopes that this uprising may be put down with as little bloodshed as possible. I know that you concur with me in wishing to rid New Mexico forever of these elements of destruction. Gentlemen — *amigos mios* — are you ready?"

Stepping forward, Don Santiago Abreu, a former departmental chief justice, saluted his governor and made reply as the spokesman for all who were gathered there. *"Mi Gobernador,* we are ready. Where you go, you will find us by your side. We know that what we face is uncertain but we also know that until our principles govern the life of this land, there will be no real or lasting peace in New Mexico. Yes, we are ready. On to Santa Cruz de la Cañada. Por Dios y la Patria."

Sounds of impatience were heard from the plaza causing Don Albino to speak hurriedly to his companions. "Thank you, Don Santiago, my thanks to all of you. I appreciate your words of loyalty and I know that they come from your hearts. I will join you in the *portal* as soon as I have said farewell to my family."

This was a difficult duty for the governor. Doña Trinidad was already prostrated and needed her husband's reassurances. There was not a young or able-bodied man left in the Palace, since all were needed in the militia. He was leaving everything in the hands of Doña Guadalupe, a woman of great courage who would be equal to any occasion.

When the governor withdrew, his supporters joined the military forces waiting in the plaza. They included the three Abreu brothers, Don Santiago, Don Ramón and Don Marcelino, as well as Don Jesús María Alarid, Don Loreto Romero and Don Miguel Sena, together with two veteran members of the New Mexico guard, Lieutenant Pedro Madrigal and Sergeant Arturo Sais. In their hands was the future of New Mexico.

Within a short time, Don Albino emerged from his wife's quarters where Doña Trinidad, fearing the worst, was reduced to complete helplessness. Of the entire household only the sleeping

Demetrio seemed unconcerned for the fate of New Mexico and its governor. Doña Guadalupe was able to accompany her nephew to the main entrance of the Palace. She knew that this was no time to collapse, although she was deeply frightened and greatly alarmed as she viewed the miniature army in the plaza. "Válgame Dios," the old lady muttered to herself, "there may be thousands of those revolutionaries waiting in the north."

It was now time to say good-bye and she knew that it would help if she remained calm. Tears could come later, though few had ever seen this Spartan woman cry. Doña Guadalupe kept her emotions to herself despite her Latin heritage.

"Courage, *tía mía*," urged Don Albino, as he embraced her. "Indians are not disciplined fighters and they have not been trained as soldiers. We will win an early victory. It is high time, and you will agree with me, that these uprisings are stopped. When peace and harmony reign in Santa Fe, you will laugh at the fears which are yours today. This is a civilized country and we must rid ourselves of this constant danger from the Indians."

"If I could only know that you would return safely, I could send you off with a smile, my Albino," whispered Doña Guadalupe.

"Of course, I will return — tomorrow, or possibly tonight," Don Albino replied. "I am only glad that in my absence, my family is in your capable hands. Believe me, *tía mía,* this is a great source of comfort to me. And you must not worry."

"I would not worry so much had I not witnessed an omen when I came from Mass this morning," she said. "A blackbird was flying around Trinidad's bedroom when I went in to see how she was. The bird had flown in through a window which had been left open by that worthless Hermenejildo. He knows that the night air is dangerous, and now we will have bad luck, all because of his carelessness. I knew it was a mistake to bring him with us to New Mexico. My father said in Veracruz fifty years ago that Hermenejildo would come to no good end."

The governor smiled as he patted his aunt's shoulder, "You and your superstitions! You have listened too much to Prudencia and Piedad and their wild tales of evil omens, flying birds and other symbols of illness and death. Forget the bird in Trinidad's bedroom. Only the unlettered believe in these signs. Look upon it all as just another indication of Hermenejildo's carelessness. You would never have consented to leave him behind in Durango. I am sure that, regardless of your threats, you will always look after him.

"And now, *tía mía*," continued Don Albino, as he endeavored to control his emotions, "if something should happen, not that it will, look after my wife and my son. They are weak and your strength is well known." Knowing that he must say no more but wishing, if at all possible, to leave on a cheerful note, Don Albino adjusted his cloak, fastened his sword more securely and in a whisper, added, "Farewell. Remember, better days will come. I hope to return soon. For the present, *adios — hasta luego*." And he was gone.

Forcing herself to remain outwardly calm, Doña Guadalupe stepped to the *portal* of the Palace and watched with a sinking heart as the military forces of New Mexico, pitifully small in numbers, moved out of the plaza. At the head of the men was their leader, Don Albino Pérez, a magnificent sight to behold for he was every inch a Mexican aristocrat. But Doña Guadalupe's heart was sad.

CHAPTER IX

A Lost Cause

In the four centuries of New Mexico's turbulent history, much of which has been replete with bloodshed and tragedy, events never transpired with such speed as in the forty-eight hours which followed Don Albino's departure from Santa Fe at the head of his army.

Arriving at San Ildefonso, where the insurgents had assembled, the governor discovered that his forces were so far outnumbered that even a pretense of engaging in battle was futile. Much of his hastily-assembled militia, when they saw the numerous Indian tribes merging as one, refused to have any part in what was so evidently a lost cause. Some gave themselves up willingly, while others, notably the Santo Domingans, actually offered their services to the enemy. The few men who chose to stand by Don Albino were truly the bravest men to ever take part in such a campaign. Desert they would not because they were not cowards. Fight they could not, not against that huge army of inflamed revolutionists. The *Perezistas* did make a small attempt by sending an occasional cannon shell into the opposing forces. This, too, was a futile action which brought a volley of arrows and simply increased the number of dead and dying. There was only one course open for honorable men on that August day in 1837 and they took it. They fled for their lives. Don

Santiago had been captured, but his two brothers, Ramón and Marcelino, together with Jesús María Alarid, were able to join their ill-fated leader in a wild and frantic effort to leave that section of New Mexico.

Don Albino knew that New Mexico was large in area. Just how big not even he knew, since the boundary lines had never been well defined. While northern New Mexico was against him and his administration, he felt that surely in those peaceful villages to the south, he would find the welcome which he had received when he first came to the territory. But first he must get to Santa Fe. He had heard the wild threats made against the members of his family and his ardent wish was that he might reach the Palace and, if at all possible, take them with him to some place of refuge. Where, he did not know. While it might not be wise even to try to evacuate his family, Don Albino felt that at least he must warn them and all the Santa Fe *Perezistas,* already waiting for him to make his victorious entry into *La Villa Real.*

And so Don Albino slipped into Santa Fe in the dark hours of the night. He and his family held a hurried and whispered conference, endeavoring to make plans though any sort of planning seemed impossible. All of the young men who had been a part of the Palace household had been drafted into the Pérez forces and not even the governor knew what fate they might have met. Doña Trinidad felt that with Santa Fe holding so many of her flesh and blood, they should at least count on some help from the Trujillo clan. Don Albino agreed to this as he looked at his frightened young wife and realized that her marriage to him had made her an alien in her own home city. Not even the Trujillo and Fernández families had all remained in the Pérez fold.

Knowing that he must be out of Santa Fe before daylight, he bade them all farewell, wondering in his heart if he would ever see them again. "Alma de mi alma," spoke the unhappy Don Albino to his wife, "choose some of your relatives who have been neutral in the political strife of this city. Surely you will find someone who will care for you now. And in their charity, I pray that they will also give refuge to my aunt and my son, as well as to those servants whom we brought to New Mexico. The enmity of the anti-*Perezistas* is against me. It should not be directed against the rest of my family and the members of my household. Good-bye. Pray for me." With these words, the Governor of New Mexico, heartsick and uncertain, rode once more out of Santa Fe, this time forever.

53

The Pérez family huddled in one room of the Palace for the rest of the night, desolate and afraid. They did try to appear calm for the benefit of the servants, now struck dumb with terror. The faithful Heremenejildo came and went constantly with bulletins of what was going on in the streets of the capital city. No one on the outside paid any attention to this *anciano,* slow witted as he was, but the old servant seemed actually to grow more and more alert as he sensed the importance of the responsibilities which were his on that night of uncertainty. He knew that, in a sense, he was paying a debt. The Pérez and Abrigo families had always been kind to him, and here was his chance to do something for them. This he did willingly and gladly, with no thought of possible danger to himself.

Old Doña Guadalupe's mind was working fast. She was trying to decide what course to follow. She knew that it was up to her to make the decisions. With the news that the insurrectionists were expected to enter Santa Fe and bring reprisals on everyone connected with the Pérez administration, she knew that it would be impossible to hide the entire Pérez household. It had been decided that Doña Trinidad would go to some of her own people and Doña Guadalupe had extracted a promise from some of the Santa Fe servants that they would merge the terrified Prudencia and Piedad into their own clans. She was not really concerned for these women because *peones* seemed to have an innate sense of danger and an equally innate talent for self-preservation. This left only the little Demetrio, and Doña Guadalupe knew that he, as the only son of the governor against whom the revolt was being staged, was the one most in danger. And, of course, he was the most helpless. Slowly but surely, plans began to form in the old lady's mind. She knew that as a woman, and an old woman at that, she could not carry out her plans singlehandedly. After much thought she decided upon the only person who might help her, Hermenejildo. Thus did Doña Guadalupe, whose life had been relatively uneventful until now, enter upon the stage of New Mexico history. There she enacted a role in a drama which has been discussed in Santa Fe until the present day.

At dawn she slipped out of a little-used door of the Palace with a basket over her arm. The basket was heavy and difficult for Doña Guadalupe to handle easily, but she hoped that this fact was not evident. She had never carried any sort of bundle on the streets of Santa Fe but she knew she must carry this basket herself. Always within sight was the faithful Hermenejildo. No humble attendant now, he realized that he was a combination of spy, scout, protector and bodyguard, not for one person but for two. Hermenejildo also had his part in the drama of Santa Fe in 1837 and he played his role well.

CHAPTER X

Sanctuary and Insurrection

Doña Guadalupe may or may not have heard of the old religious doctrine of "Sanctuary." This was an arrangement by which anyone fleeing from danger might enter a religious edifice and find not only shelter but immunity from capture. At any rate, she decided that a church would be the ideal place for the concealment of little Demetrio Pérez. She felt that there was little hope that the insurrectionists would respect any building, even one devoted to religious purposes. But even so, she could think of no better place for her grandnephew than the upper gallery in the rear of the Church of San Miguel. This venerable temple of God had been almost destroyed in the Pueblo Revolt of 1680 and rebuilt some years later by other Indians. Doña Guadalupe prayed for her fleeing nephew and hoped that somewhere in the wilderness Don Albino had found for himself a "Sanctuary."

Not daring to remain long in the upper gallery since this would arouse suspicion in those who might discover her, Doña Guadalupe knelt in one of the rear pews of the Church of San Miguel. She voiced her prayers but her mind was naturally distracted. She was always listening for a sound which might come from the sleeping

baby overhead. She kept this up all day and when dusk descended on the ancient city, she felt that she could venture out with safety. Little Demetrio had been fed and was sound asleep. He was a healthy child and it was safe to assume that he would not waken until morning.

Seating herself on the steps near the shadowed entrance of the church, Doña Guadalupe relaxed. She even felt a sense of security. The moon was full on that August night, but it was dark enough for her to feel concealed. She hoped that anyone passing would accept her as just another one of the old women who were accustomed to rest in the shadows of the church during the evening hours. And many did pass that way, and their talk was all of the insurrection, the danger in which they moved, whether or not Santa Fe would fall before this onslaught from the north, and what of the fate of New Mexico's governor? By now, all of Santa Fe knew that Don Albino had ridden out of the city in the early morning hours.

Suddenly old Doña Guadalupe realized that she was very tired. Mingled sentiments went through her mind and heart as she sat in the darkness, waiting for Hermenejildo to return with information about the women in the Palace. She wasted very little time on being afraid. Neither did she indulge in self-pity. There were times, however, when she couldn't help but wonder at a destiny which had transplanted her to this isolated outpost. And having been transplanted, why had she been confronted with nothing but trouble? Hate was really uppermost in her mind, and Doña Guadalupe wished that she could erase this feeling from her thoughts. She hated Santa Fe and its narrow streets, the monotonous buildings, the political intrigue and the constant danger in which they, as the first family of the land, had been forced to move since the time of their arrival from Mexico. She knew that her nephew had known no peace of mind in the twenty-eight months he had served as governor of New Mexico. Even his philanthropic ideas had brought him nothing but grief and disappointment. He also was unpopular and in this Doña Guadalupe knew that she herself shared. Never one to cater to others, she knew now that she had not bothered much about New Mexico and New Mexicans and that in this neglect, she had been wrong. She should have done more to enhance the position of the Pérez family in New Mexico. In fact, she had often wondered if Don Albino's subjects were worth all the trouble he took in their behalf. Certainly they had shown him no gratitude. Yes, she hated Santa Fe. She could not seem to help it.

Hearing footsteps and recognizing them as the shuffling gait of Hermenejildo, she eagerly awaited his arrival. But even in the darkness, she could sense that something was wrong. Hermenejildo's features were a mask of horror. He couldn't say a word. Doña Guadalupe begged and cajoled and threatened the old man but with no results. Hermenejildo had seen sights on the plaza and on the road to Rosario Chapel upon which men are seldom called to look. The experience had literally shocked him out of his senses. Doña Guadalupe finally realized his state of mind and forcing the old man to sit on the church steps, she hurried toward the plaza.

As she moved carefully down the darkened streets, the echoes of an unearthly commotion grew more and more distinct. She was afraid, but she had to find out what was going on. From Hermenejildo's condition she feared the worst. And well she might, for soon after Doña Guadalupe crossed the Santa Fe plaza, which itself was shrouded in an eerie silence, she beheld a sight that froze her blood. Beyond the plaza to the west of the Palace she could see *La Capilla de Nuestra Señora del Rosario,* built originally as the fulfillment of a vow by Don Diego de Vargas Zapata Lujan Ponce de Leon. This sacred ground was now the encampment of the *insurrectos.* The scene was one of pandemonium and gross sacrilege. In the realization of what had happened she was like someone turned to stone. For once in her life Doña Guadalupe Abrigo was rendered completely helpless.

On and on rode numerous Indians and Spanish rebels, all mounted on horses and all screaming and howling in an inhuman manner. Since many of them carried flaming torches, the old lady could see the participants well. One of their number, a wild young man, was uttering hyena-like screams and holding aloft a lance. Something round was attached to the tip of the spear. It waved just above the flare of the torches. Doña Guadalupe, hidden by the shadows, moved closer in an attempt to learn what the rebels were about. Just then the young horseman dipped his lance toward a group of laughing comrades. Illuminated by the flames of the torches was the head of Don Albino Pérez, *hidalgo* of New Spain, Colonel of the Durango militia, Governor of New Mexico.

Much later Doña Guadalupe was to wonder at her own reaction to that moment. She did not become hysterical or scream or faint. She stood perfectly still in the darkness and muttered over and over, "Holy Mary, Mother of God, pray for us . . ." How long she remained was another mystery to her.

Eventually she realized that her strength was returning, and she knew that she must go. Overcoming a desire to faint and an even stronger desire to die, she made her way back to the plaza and crossed it. She glanced toward the Palace and noticed that it was in darkness, and all the doors were open. Would she ever see Doña Trinidad or her faithful servants again? She breathed a prayer for Trinidad and all who dwelt there. She realized that there was nothing she, a lone woman, could do for them, and sadly accepted the fact there was nothing she could now do for Don Albino. His life had come to an end and with it her own lifetime of devotion to the orphaned boy. She could only pray for his soul. But not for her the luxury of giving up. There still remained the baby Demetrio in the balcony of San Miguel. Though tired and brokenhearted, her mind cleared and she knew that now more than ever Demetrio was her chief responsibility. With stumbling and faltering footsteps, she made her way back to the church.

As she neared the church, she was gratified to see that Hermenejildo was waiting for her. At least, the faithful old *peon* was alive and she could lean on him. She had no one else in this unhappy city, no one to turn to, or so it seemed to the lonely old woman.

Upon reaching the church, fear seized Doña Guadalupe again as she realized that Hermenejildo was not alone. However, she was immediately reassured as the old servant, having regained his speech, came to meet her. He, too, was relieved to see that Doña Guadalupe knew the worst and was still able to go on. If she was all right, then everything else in the world was all right. Doña Guadalupe would see to that, he reasoned. Wherever she went and whatever she decided to do, he would accept her word. Maybe they could leave this city in the north and return to Veracruz. He had already travelled too many miles and seen too much. However, he knew that the decision would not be his but Doña Guadalupe's, and when the decision was made, he would be glad to follow. This he had done for fifty years, and he knew no other way.

And so, doffing his decrepit hat, even in the midst of tragedy this humble old man was not one to forget his manners in the presence of his betters, he almost hurried as he said, "Do not be afraid, Doña Guadalupe, we have a friend. *El Vicario* is here."

CHAPTER XI

A Friend Among Enemies

Coming forward and holding out his hands, both in greeting and as a gesture of support to the old woman, was the ranking prelate of the Church in Santa Fe, the Very Reverend Juan Felipe Ortiz, the representative of the distant Bishop of Durango.

"Come, my good woman," said the Vicar, "I welcome you and I rejoice that you, at least, are unharmed. I have been in the gallery of the church, and I am happy to be able to inform you that your grandnephew is safe and well and asleep. You were wise to leave the Palace and bring the child here to the safety of God's house. Your servant tells me that you have been to Rosario. I can tell that you have seen for yourself what is going on there. I join you in your grief because your illustrious nephew was my friend. I pray that his soul may find the peace which New Mexico failed to give him."

He paused for a few moments knowing that he had to say more to strengthen Doña Guadalupe for the days ahead. Then the Vicar continued, "In time, Doña Guadalupe, you will find comfort in the fact that Don Albino will go down in history as a great and unselfish man, a man who was possibly ahead of his time but, nevertheless, a statesman. He gave his life for New Mexico, a land which gave him very little happiness. As a lifelong resident of this city, I regret that this was so, and I almost feel I must apologize for my own people, especially since you, too, have shared in this unhappiness. In view of this, I shall also pray that you may keep bitterness from your heart.''

For the first time in many hours Doña Guadalupe was able to find her voice. She replied to the Vicar, ''Thank you, Reverend Father, I am grateful for your kind words. My loss is great, and it will be years before the burden is lifted. Albino was my life. He was like my own son, and I wish that my life might have been taken and his spared. Yes, he had many troubles here in New Mexico but he loved the people of this region. It was not given him to remain here long enough to carry out his plans but who knows, maybe it was his place to sow the seed and for others to reap the harvest. My nephew encountered much opposition, and his enemies were unfair. Despite all this, there was never hatred in his heart. And I know, Reverend Father, that I will never be happy until I have erased bitterness from my own heart.''

Doña Guadalupe gained control of her emotions before continuing. ''But what of my nephew's wife? And of those poor women I brought from Mexico to this unhappy land? What shall little Demetrio and I do now? We can not go on, day after day, in that gallery. And old Hermenejildo, what is to become of him? Tell me, Reverend Father, what am I to do?

The Vicar of Santa Fe had been wondering himself what course these refugees should follow. In answer to Doña Guadalupe's frantic questions he said, ''I think, good Doña Guadalupe, that I can help you. Out on the Pecos Trail I have some friends who can be trusted. They were also friends of your nephew but they were never listed definitely as *Perezistas*. They have taken very little part in the political strife which has been rampant here in Santa Fe, and in their house you will find safety. At least, you will be safer than anywhere else. Their home is simple but in it you will find a welcome, you and little Demetrio. There will also be a place for Hermenejildo. Here in the city, we are all in danger. Therefore, it is best that you remain only for the rest of the night here in the church. By morning, we will know what the situation is on the plaza. If safe, my driver will be here at dawn and he will be waiting in the street which runs along the side of the church. He knows how to reach this house on the Pecos Trail, and since he is completely trustworthy, you will be quite safe in his hands. His name is Fidel, and he has already risked his life many times in the cause of justice. I will communicate with you when there is news. Once you reach the home of my friends, do try to relax and get some rest.''

As Doña Guadalupe started to reply, the good Vicar stopped her, ''No, do not try to thank me. I see that you accept my suggestions. Please be ready when Fidel arrives, for it will be best if you are out of Santa Fe and on the road before sunrise.''

Opening one of the massive doors of San Miguel Church, the Vicar held it for Doña Guadalupe to enter, at the same time, saying, ''And now I must go. Before I leave you, let us pray to the only certain source we have, Almighty God. We will pray for your safety and for the soul of Don Albino. And I ask that you pray for our unhappy city, that peace may one day come to Santa Fe. And do not forget to pray for the many who died with Don Albino. They all gave their lives for New Mexico.''

The Vicar of Santa Fe approached the altar of the old mission church, and Doña Guadalupe followed him until she reached one of the pews near the altar railing. There she was glad to sink to her knees. As she prayed, she was aware of a feeling of peace and gratitude, gratitude that she could now follow the directions of someone else. Tired and sick, heartbroken and lonely, she had walked alone too long. Responsibility had worn her out.

''My Lord and my God'' were the words which came to her lips. They also came from her heart. She looked long and steadily at the altar of San Miguel Mission Church, where the sanctuary lamp had been burning for almost two centuries.

CHAPTER XII

A Refuge on the Old Pecos Trail

Five months passed. In many ways, they were good for Doña Guadalupe. For the first time in her long life she tasted the joys of simple people. Completely dependent upon her host, she was sensible enough to fit her life, as well as the lives of the infant Demetrio and Hermenejildo, into the daily pattern of Pedro Mondragón and his family. She was surprised to find how easy it was to do without the many comforts which she had always felt were essential. Veracruz and Durango, and yes, even Santa Fe, receded in importance as the old Mexican aristocrat tried to make herself useful. Fortunately she was an excellent seamstress, and before long the daughters of the Mondragón household were blossoming forth in remodeled wardrobes. Demetrio grew as he had never grown in the old Palace of the Governors, and old Hermenejildo, a born handyman, was probably the most useful of the three refugees.

Doña Gauadalupe knew, however, that this couldn't go on forever but at the suggestion of the Vicar of Santa Fe, she awaited the day when things became more settled in Santa Fe. When that

day came, she would make plans. She did toy a little with the idea of returning to Mexico but Doña Guadalupe was out of touch with her homeland, and she felt that there her future might be even more precarious. General Santa Ana had fallen from power and was, for the time being, living in exile. The òne-legged dictator of Mexico had dictated too long and too ruthlessly. The Republic, always ready for a change in rulers, had witnessed his retirement after the defeat of the Mexicans by the Texans at San Jacinto. Unwilling to live out his days in the empty glory which is the lot of fallen despots, the General was busily engaged in plots and plans to rise once more to a position of influence and power. The outcome was uncertain, and therefore Doña Guadalupe reasoned that Mexico was not for her. Her native borders were closed to her and the baby in her charge. Revolutions were always imminent in Mexico and insurrections equally imminent in New Mexico. Doña Guadalupe found it hard to make a choice, so for the time being, it seemed best to stay where she was.

During her first weeks at the house on the Pecos Trail, Doña Guadalupe had received more sad news. The Mondragón family was able to glean bits of information from travelers, information that only added to her burden. She learned the details of the rebellion and the subsequent tragedy that befell all *Perezistas*.

When Don Albino left the Palace on the morning of August the Ninth, he and his companions had headed toward the Rio Grande and the *Camino Real*. Their thought, apparently, was to reach the friendly settlements south of Alburquerque as it was doubtful that they could make the journey to Mexico in their ill-prepared condition.

It soon became obvious to them that they were being followed by insurgents. What they did not know, but probably guessed, was that the villages and pueblos along the river had been alerted to seize and hold the fleeing party. Don Albino decided that the only hope lay in splitting up with each man seeking his own escape. Sending his horse on with a friend, Pérez started for Santa Fe on foot.

Late that night he reached the home of Don Salvador Martínez in the tiny village of Agua Fria, a league from the Santa Fe plaza. There he stopped for water and a brief rest. Just as he was about to continue his journey several Santo Domingo Indians, who had been following him all day, leapt out of hiding and riddled his body with lances. Even before he had breathed his last one of the band severed his head from his body. With shouts of victory the Indians rode off to Santa Fe with their bloody trophy on the tip of a lance. Don Albino's mutilated body was left behind in the dust of Agua Fria.

Don Albino was not the only one to give his life for New Mexico that day. Don Jesús María Alarid, the departmental secretary, had been stripped of his clothing, pierced with lances and left to die alone on the arid wastes not far from where his leader had met a similar fate. All three of the Abreu brothers had perished. Don Ramon and Don Marcelino had met their deaths quickly but no such kindly fate was in store for Don Santiago. He was compelled to submit to one of the cruelest deaths recored in the annals of Indian massacres. This brave *hidalgo,* once a govenor and later a chief justice of New Mexico, was captured and dragged to the pueblo of Santo Domingo, where he was placed in stocks for the night. In the morning, his hands, feet, arms and legs were cut off with savage deliberation. Death was a welcome release. As nearly as Doña Guadalupe could ascertain, not one of Don Albino's supporters was left alive.

Saddest of all the tragedy which surrounded the death of Don Albino was the fact that Doña Trinidad was nowhere to be found. She had disappeared from the Palace and from Santa Fe. Doña Guadalupe could accept death; she had done that many times. Even the tragic deaths of her nephew and his followers had a touch of finality. It was over and done with. She mourned for them, but they had died for an ideal. Their days of turmoil and strife were behind them. They had laid down their burdens and she felt that they were already reaping their rewards in a better world, in a world where bloodshed and revolutions were unknown. But Doña Trinidad's fate — that was another matter. Where was she? What had happened to the wife of the governor in that night of terror? No one knew the answers.

The government in Santa Fe, Doña Guadalupe knew, was a fiasco and had been so for five months. With the liquidation of all the influential *Perezistas,* Don Manuel Armijo emerged once more into the limelight. It was expected that he would do this and that he would take over completely. However, the despot from Alburquerque was given a temporary set-back. Ironically, it was Armijo himself who insisted on the election of a new governor. When the ballots were counted, it was found that José Gonzales was the duly elected governor of New Mexico. And so Manuel Armijo, having presumably staged the whole revolution, was confronted with the necessity for bringing about a counter-revolution. This sort of thing could always be accomplished by Don Manuel Armijo. He knew how and when to pull the strings.

Governor Gonzales left for Taos one day to look after his sheep. On his return trip to the capital he was met in Santa Cruz by the Armijo forces and detained. Armijo, who had not received the recognition he felt he deserved, had already set himself up as a combination of *commandante general, gobernador* and *jefe político* with the backing of a sizable force of soldiers. New Mexico, reasoned Don Manuel, was not big enough for two governors, so the only solution was to have José Gonzales shot. Armijo had made this move all very legal by announcing the *Plan de Tomé* which in effect made Gonzales the rebel and Armijo the rightful governor.

Those who witnessed the shooting marveled at the Indian's bravery. He had successfully united numerous Indian tribes and led an invasion of Santa Fe at the instigation of Armijo and his cohorts. He had served his purpose. He knew more than he should, so he was executed in the plaza of stormy Santa Cruz de la Cañada without a trial. There were some who protested, but Armijo assured them that there was nothing he could do. His hands were tied. It was the will of the people. José Gonzales was little more than a brave puppet, a tragic puppet in a tragic era. He belonged to the open mesas and was only at home on a horse, riding fearlessly into wild herds of buffalo. Dangerous though this vocation was, José Gonzales would probably have lived to a ripe and honored old age as a buffalo hunter had circumstances not made him the acknowledged leader of the *revolucionarios*. He certainly never expected to occupy the Palace of the Governors in Santa Fe but it was there that destiny placed him, short though his tenure was. His role in history was doomed; it ended in a pool of blood in Santa Cruz.

Numerous others also lost their lives. They knew too much, or in some instances were too ambitious, one condition being about as dangerous as the other in 1837. Power was reserved for one man in the New Mexico of the 1830's, Don Manuel Armijo.

Not even Diego Esquibel escaped. The former *alcalde* was unimportant. His original crime was that he was prejudiced in favor of his relatives and that he had allowed this fact to influence his official life. This action provided one of the sparks which ignited the revolution of 1837. He too, had served his purpose. He was a menace to the future, so he was murdered. And since all his *primos* were loyal to him as he had been to them, they followed him to his grave.

Strangely enough, all this endless trouble had failed to make Doña Guadalupe Abrigo's position in Santa Fe insecure. Ordinarily, she and little Demetrio might have felt the iron hand of Don Manuel Armijo, since they surely epitomized everything connected with the Pérez cause. That this was not the case was because Santa Fe itself had undergone a change of heart. Now that Don Albino and his administration, his ideals, and his plans were a thing of the past, the residents of the capital city began to see what manner of man Don Albino Pérez had been. The hearts of these sympathetic Latins went out to his aging aunt and helpless son. A little late, but nevertheless, they meant to be kind, and now they were anxious to help the family of the man for whose blood they had been calling in the preceding summer.

· Don Manuel was aware of this growing sentiment, and since he had risen to power again and again through compromise and political trades, he sensed that it would be a splendid thing to guarantee safety to the members of the Pérez family. He knew that his political position was not as strong as it had once been and that those in power in Mexico were a bit doubtful as to Don Manuel's role in New Mexico's troubles. He had set himself up as an emancipator but many knew the actual part he had played in planning the revolution of 1837. And so the restored governor decided that it would be highly expedient to see that no harm came to Doña Guadalupe and little Demetrio. At any rate, what possible danger could come to him from an old woman and an infant boy? Don Manuel could afford to be generous.

Doña Guadalupe knew all this, and while her fierce and dominant Abrigo pride would once have made her refuse any concessions from one so patently an enemy, she knew that her days of dominance were over. It was no longer her place to reject. Even a little expedience on her part might be wise. Her sole interest now was in little Demetrio, that he might grow up a worthy descendant of his illustrious ancestors. And so she began again to make plans. Some semblance of order was being restored to Santa Fe and this seemed to be the best place for her to settle. She knew of a house which belonged to a member of Father Ortiz' family that she could have. She had imposed on the Mondragón family long enough. For a number of months, they had stretched their meager resources to include the care of three additional people. They had done enough.

Once again the vicar's carriage drove to Doña Guadalupe's refuge on the Pecos Trail and once again the loyal Fidel took care of transferring the Pérez family to new surroundings. Snow had been falling for many days and a blizzard seemed imminent, but he hoped to cover the three miles to Santa Fe before nightfall.

On the bitterly cold day in January of 1838 Fidel was finding it difficult to steer his horses through what was already a blinding snow storm. It hardly seemed possible that less than three years before Doña Guadalupe had entered the same capital in semi-royal state as a part of the governor's caravan.

She looked back at the Mondragón household and thanked God that for a little while she had been allowed to know complete peace and quiet and the companionship of unselfish friends. They had asked for nothing from her as she had very little to give. The days ahead might be uncertain, but Doña Guadalupe was prepared for whatever might come. She had learned a lot in the little house on the Pecos Trail.

CHAPTER XIII

Life on the Analco

El Barrio de Analco, or "The Analco," as the neighborhood was commonly referred to in Santa Fe, was not an exclusive part of the capital city. Originally started as a place of residence for the servants of the *ricos* of Santa Fe, most of whom lived on the north side of the river or adjacent to the *Parroquia* of St. Francis, the Analco was distinctly a part of the city but certainly not a place of abode for the *gente fina.* It was in this section that Doña Guadalupe and little Demetrio found themselves, "on the wrong side of the river." In the old days of pomp and glory, Doña Guadalupe would have scoffed at the idea that she might end her days amidst lesser people, simple folk who did not seem to mind their location. They were happy and carefree and gay. They had their own *fiestas,* their *bailes* and their own place of worship — the Mission Church of San Miguel, dear to Doña Guadalupe's heart since it had figured so prominently in her life on a former occasion.

Eight years went by and the old woman grew to love El Barrio de Analco. It mattered little that the area was not an exclusive one. Her neighbors were kindly and generous when they had anything to give. Down the street was the *curandera* for the whole Analco and many times, when Doña Guadalupe's joints were aching with the *reuma,* the herbs and liquid potions of the *curandera* had eased her

pains. Satisfied as to her own background, birth and breeding, Doña Guadalupe was sensible enough to know that neighborhoods and surroundings could not alter the fact that in Veracruz and in Durango she had been of "the right people."

Doña Guadalupe grew to love the little house which belonged to the Ortiz family. She had become well established as a seamstress and was now able to pay a small rental, which the *vicario* accepted since he knew that it gave the old aristocrat satisfaction and a feeling of independence. That she had never lacked for employment was partly because Doña Guadalupe had grown into an almost legendary figure in the capital city. Curiosity alone brought some of the carriages of Santa Fe's socially elect to her door, thus enabling inquisitive women to see for themselves the aging aristocrat who had once been the First Lady of New Mexico. They were equally anxious, of course, to see the former governor's son, now growing into a handsome Mexican lad. His polished manners, which might have fitted a grown *hidalgo* more than a boy of ten, were a joy to these women who represented the elect of Santa Fe. Of a studious and musical nature, little Demetrio's blue eyes reflected the temperament of both attributes. Even at this early age, he showed much promise.

Out of trouble and bloodshed and sorrow, the two refugees had remade their lives and were really quite happy in their four-room house. For a time, old Hermenejildo had been a part of the household but he missed the fields and the growing things which he had come to love on the Mondragón farm. There Hermenejildo had discovered that he had a peculiar knack for growing vegetables. He had also cared for the fruit trees in the Mondragón orchards. As a result the apples from these orchards were in great demand in the Santa Fe market, located in the *portal* of the Palace of the Governors. He felt that all of these produces were really his own creation. Doña Guadalupe knew this, so when *Señor* Pedro Mondragón came down with continued spells of the *fiebre*, she sent Hermenejildo out to assist on the *rancho*. When the Mondragóns asked him to remain permanently, the old servant was torn between what he considered to be his duty to his *patrona* and his love for the rural things of the Pecos Trail. Urged on by his mistress, he gave in to his second allegiance, and, thus, another link with the past was severed in the life of Doña Guadalupe Abrigo.

Fortunately for the old woman who had always been accustomed to servants, Prudencia found her way back to Santa Fe not long after Doña Guadalupe settled in the Analco. Her joy at being reunited with her former mistress was pitiful to see. It was evident that Prudencia had been through trials and experiences which had all but robbed her of her reason. Knowing that the old maidservant had been stolen by Indians, Doña Guadalupe treated it as a closed chapter and made every effort to help the poor soul back to happiness and sanity. As for Piedad, they learned that she had fared even worse. She had first been enslaved, then sold and finally murdered in cold blood for the entertainment of a Comanche squaw.

But still there was no word from Doña Trinidad. It was rumored that she had been seen on the west side of the river near Alburquerque but that town was far away, and Doña Guadalupe had no means of tracing the reports. Frequently, Doña Guadalupe and little Demetrio went to the Shrine of Our Lady of Guadalupe, farther along the river, and burned vigil lights for the welfare of the boy's mother. They also lighted candles for Piedad, that her soul might find peace, and Doña Guadalupe did not forget to thank God for the safe return of Prudencia. Busy with her patterns, scissors and threads, she needed help and was grateful for the fact that at least her household could boast of one servant.

The refugees had experienced a struggle in their first years in the Analco. Governor Armijo had left them alone but they were never quite certain of their security. In view of this, they were not sorry when they heard of Don Manuel's recall from the Santa Fe scene, especially since it became their privilege and delight to become well acquainted with his successor, General Mariano Martínez de Lejanza, and his gifted and beautiful wife, Doña Teresita. They, too, were Mexicans, and to Doña Guadalupe they were someone from home.

Coming to Doña Guadalupe to have her already lavish wardrobe replenished, Doña Teresita was surprised to find that the old seamstress had actually preceded her by a few years as the mistress of the Palace of Governors. She interested her husband in the Pérez family, and it was not long before Don Mariano was taking a genuine interest in the orphan son of his predecessor. He delighted in talking to Demetrio and found pleasure in the boy's adult outlook and in his classical Spanish.

Don Mariano, like those who had gone before him, was having his troubles in New Mexico and it rested and relaxed him to spend long hours with Doña Guadalupe and the boy Demetrio. The old woman could never bring herself to accept invitations to the Palace, and so their hours of social contact and endless conversation about

74

their homeland, New Mexico politics, Santa Fe gossip and little Demetrio's education, all took place in Doña Guadalupe's little house. Great excitement reigned among the humble folk in the Barrio de Analco when the governor's magnificent carriage, drawn by impatient and spirited horses, arrived at the house of their illustrious neighbor.

Determined that Demetrio should not grow up entirely in the midst of sewing operations, Doña Guadalupe devoted only one of her four rooms to her means of livelihood. In this back room she kept her materials and all the equipment necessary to a seamstress. With the eviction of the Pérez family from the Palace, they had lost all of the beautiful and rare furnishings which they had brought from Mexico. Everything had been confiscated, even Don Albino's fine broadcloths and imported linens. These had been worn by José Gonzales, the buffalo hunter and, for a brief time, governor of New Mexico. The Pérez jewels had been given outright to a group of American traders who claimed to have given unlimited credit to the Pérez family. Not even the red velvet draperies had been salvaged. They had once been the talk of Santa Fe and now hung in the largest gambling hall of the city, the monte salon operated by Doña Gertrudis Barcelo, whose growing wealth was transforming her into a woman of influence. However, Doña Guadalupe did not mourn for the draperies as they would hardly be appropriate for her limited quarters. She was only happy that she had been able to retrieve some of the lesser objects which she had brought from Durango. Some of these rare pieces had found their way into Santa Fe homes after the revolution and had eventually been returned to her. Assembling all these small things, she was able to make her parlor into an inviting *sala*. Prudencia had added her touch with geraniums, and Hermenejildo had brought in ferns from the Pecos Trail. As Doña Guadalupe viewed her tiny parlor, she felt that the room required no apologies.

The *pièce de resistance* was an old harpsichord. On this instrument little Demetrio played, for he had early shown an aptitude for music. True, the battered harpsichord was a bit out of tune but when he played old Spanish ballads, favorites of Doña Guadalupe's from the days of Veracruz, the old woman sat back with tears in her eyes and joy in her heart. Life was not too bad for Doña Guadalupe, and she refused to mourn for the glories of the past. After all, they had not brought her the happiness which she was finding in little Demetrio.

CHAPTER XIV
Son of Don Albino

And Demetrio himself — he was really more than happy most of the time. Through the kindness of Governor Martínez de Lejanza, he had been enrolled in a private school started in Santa Fe by Señor Eduardo Engelbert Tatty. Tatty was an Englishman but, as his Christian name indicated, a Spanish scholar with a degree from Barcelona. This school was the delight of Demetrio's life. He arose each morning, avid for what he knew the day would bring as Señor Tatty unfolded whole new worlds for the interest and edification of his students. He was also studying the violin and showed a marked talent. Since religion had a vital place in education, it was a common sight to see the boys from the Tatty school marching in precise formation, two by two, on their way to the *Parroquia* of St. Francis for their daily hour of Christian doctrine.

It looked as if Don Albino's dreams were being realized in Santa Fe. Education was becoming more easily available, and his own son was among the beneficiaries.

Demetrio had met with one special sorrow, however, and his sadness was enhanced because Don Mariano Martínez de Lejanza, his sponsor and protector, was responsible for it. Like his father, the boy was sensitive and felt things deeply. For some years, one of the familiar landmarks of Santa Fe had been a monument which rose in

the plaza to a height of fifty feet. The base was much larger than the monument itself and stood approximately five feet high. The surface of the base, reached by a series of steps, was a platform large enough for men and boys to use as a place of relaxation in the sun. Here, Demetrio and his fellow students from the Tatty school were accustomed to dream their dreams and discuss the problems which are the lot of ten year old boys. At the very crest of the monument, brilliant in its coloring and discernible from below, was a magnificent eagle with a green snake in its mouth, the Eagle of the Republic of Mexico. Since little Demetrio had heard so many times the story of his father from the lips of Doña Guadalupe and since she had also painted a glowing picture of Mexico for the boy's benefit, the monument had become a symbol to Demetrio, a symbol of everything for which his father stood. He particularly liked the Mexican eagle, which seemed to suspend itself in the azure skies which canopied Santa Fe.

But one day, as the boys from the Tatty school were nearing the plaza, they were horrified to see that workmen were razing the monument. Questioning the workmen, the boys were informed that, at the mandate of Governor Martínez de Lejanza, the monument was being removed in order that the plaza might be converted into an arena for bullfights. The wild and wiry bulls were to be kept in stalls around the plaza and Governor Martínez de Lejanza hoped that this old Spanish sport would be well received in *La Villa Real*. Of course, this excited the boys and little Demetrio, Mexican child that he was, felt especially interested. He knew all about bullfights as they had frequently figured in old Doña Guadalupe's yarns.

However enticing the prospect of bullfights, little Demetrio knew that he would miss his "Eagle in the Sky."

On top of this disappointment came another sorrow for little Demetrio in which Doña Guadalupe shared. One evening in the spring of 1845 the governor's carriage drew up at the little house in the Analco. After being settled in Doña Guadalupe's parlor, the governor and his wife informed their hostess that they were returning to Mexico. Life as a general in the armies of Mexico had been strenuous enough for Don Mariano but he had now found life in the Palace of the Governors in Santa Fe even more of a trial.

The governor had recently faced a bloody uprising of his own. A band of outlaw Navajos had been captured and brought to Santa Fe. Among the party were a number of Utes who protested their innocence and demanded their immediate release. Martínez de

Lejanza evidently did not act quickly enough or else mistook the demands for threats. Whatever the cause the executive offices of the Palace were soon turned into a battleground.

Don Mariano might have fallen victim if the alert Doña Teresita had not rushed in with his sword. She was later able to call the sentries who soon restored peace. Ironically, many of the Indians had hidden in the stalls the governor had had constructed around the plaza and from these vantage points had been able to withstand the sentries.

Though the blame for this unfortunate and bloody incident was never fully placed on Don Mariano, it was felt in Mexico that his usefulness in Santa Fe was over, and he was recalled.

He had now come to ask Doña Guadalupe and Demetrio to join them. The old lady was tempted to accept. She was growing old and had always expected to be buried in the Abrigo vault overlooking the sea above the fortified harbor of Veracruz. However, something seemed to remind her constantly that Demetrio's destiny was here in New Mexico, here in Santa Fe where he had been born. New Mexico's *cementerios* were barren graveyards, and Doña Guadalupe disliked to think that she would await the day of judgment in a grave on a lonely mesa, but if this was part of the price she must pay to enable little Demetrio to fulfill his destiny, she was willing. After all, it didn't make very much difference if her niche in the Veracruz mausoleum remained empty.

They said farewell to Don Mariano and his gracious lady. Doña Guadalupe felt that her decision to remain in Santa Fe had been a wise one. She had some doubts within a few days, however, when she heard that Don Manuel Armijo was again coming to Santa Fe as governor for the third time. Doña Guadalupe and Don Manuel had never met face to face but she knew him by sight. When she saw him on the occasion of his return in 1846, she felt that she had little to fear. Time had taken its toll of the aging despot; this was evident, and Doña Guadalupe felt that the old man had probably forgotten the existence of Don Albino Pérez' aunt and son. He had more important things to worry about.

The winter of 1846 was probably the gayest in Santa Fe during the Mexican regime. The monte tables in the gambling salons were crowded with the *ricos,* the *peones,* the military, the mountain men and the American traders, all engaged in a wild and reckless scramble to increase their American dollars or Mexican *pesos.* *Bailes* were held in the streets and stabbings and shootings were the

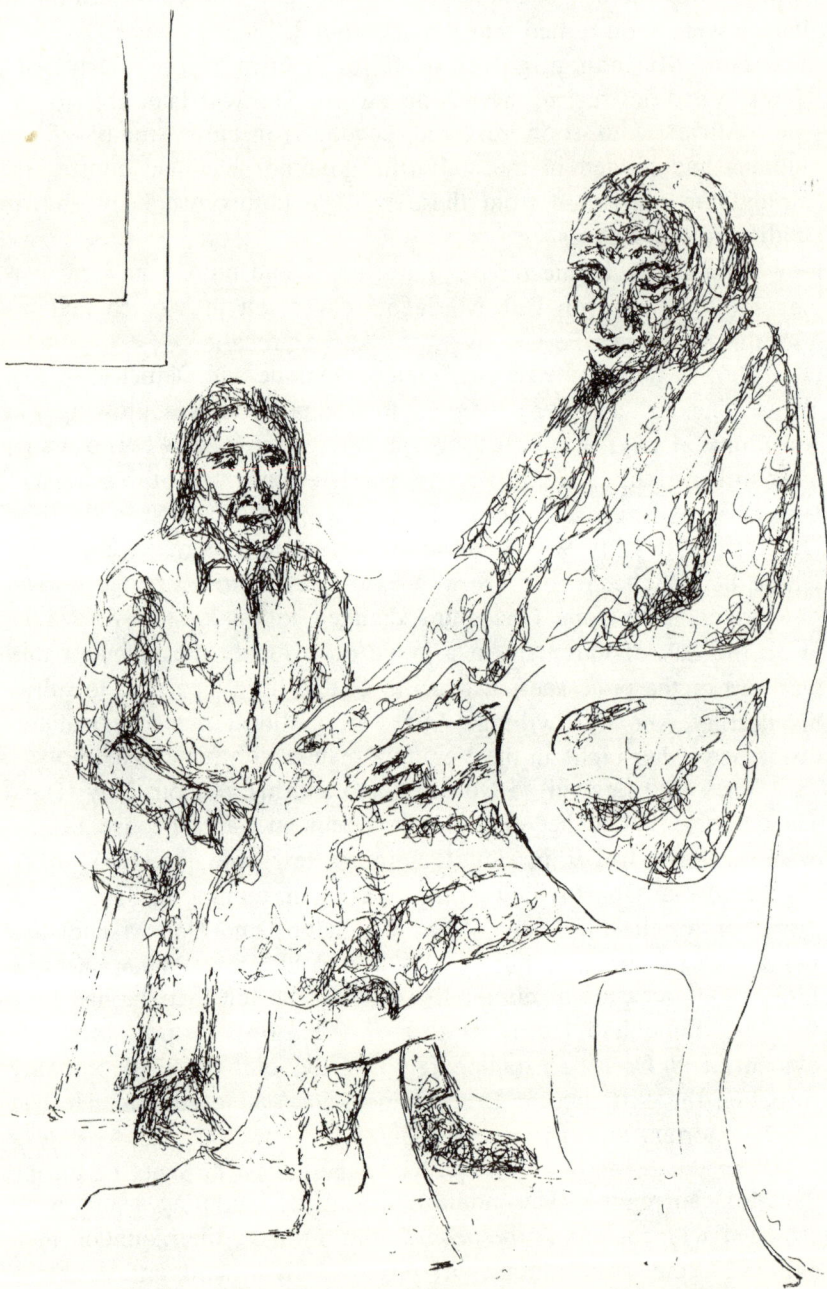

order of the day. The *alcaldes* seemed unable to preserve any sort of order, and everyone in Santa Fe appeared to be determined to live, and live riotously, each day. Something was in the air but no one knew exactly what it was. Coming and going, busier than anyone else in the capital city, was Don Santiago Magoffin. Having come to New Mexico from Kentucky many years before as plain James Magoffin, this trader seemed to know what he was doing and what was going on. It was rumored also that Don Manuel Armijo, closeted in his offices in the Palace of the Governors, was in on the secret, too.

It was a lonely winter, however, for Doña Guadalupe and little Demetrio. They remained quietly in their little *casita* in the Barrio de Analco and had no part in the mad excitement prevalent on the plaza. The *curandera* was called more frequently for Doña Guadalupe's aching joints and more and more she sent for little Demetrio and had him wring from the out-of-tune harpsichord the old ballads which she loved. She had one other diversion, the reading of Don Donaciano Vigil's weekly publication, *La Verdad*. Don Donaciano was the son of the old *alcalde* from the Rio Santa Fe, that venerable sage who had sounded the note of warning during Governor Pérez' conference on taxation long ago. Old Don Juan Cristóbal was no more but his sons were active in the life of Santa Fe. The old Judge would have welcomed *La Verdad* and the fact that his son was its editor. A journal was being published in New Mexico, and Don Albino Pérez was not there to see it, but his dreams were being realized.

Strange to say, the news for which Santa Fe was waiting with such excitement was first heard in the Analco section of the city. This was because the Santa Fe Trail, the thoroughfare which was used by trader, trapper, explorer and bandit alike in the 1840's, ran through that section of the capital city. Wagon trains and stagecoaches provided little Demetrio with thrills, and since the drivers of these vehicles were the newscasters of their day, it came about that Demetrio was one of the first in Santa Fe to hear the astounding news which soon had the whole city in the throes of fear and expectancy.

From Bent's Fort, so went the reports, General Stephen Watts Kearny and his "Army of the West" had marched on Las Vegas in northern New Mexico. General Kearny had made an impressive address to which the populace listened in the plaza. Without bloodshed or the firing of a shot, this northern New Mexico hamlet had succumbed to the general's announcement that it was now a part of the United States of America. If his listeners had any doubt as to the authenticity of his audacious statement, the general reminded them that they needed only to look at the American flag flying from a second-story balcony. The stagecoach drivers had seen it waving in the wind. It was red and white and blue and, as they remembered, had twenty-eight stars.

Little Demetrio ran to share the news with his great-aunt, news which was soon augmented by reports that the *americanos* – "the Army of the West" — were nearing El Cañoncito de los Apaches, ten miles from Santa Fe. Doña Guadalupe eased her rheumatic body into her favorite chair and gave herself up to conjecture, "Is it now my lot to witness another change in government?" She had altered her life enough, she felt, but if necessary she supposed she could do it again. To many in Santa Fe, "the Army of the West" meant the coming of the enemy, despite all this talk of liberation which came from the illustrious General Kearny. Conquering leaders always spoke in this manner, and Santa Fe residents, like conquered people down through the ages, scarcely knew what to make of it all. Little Demetrio, with no fear in his heart, sat down to wait. He had a reserved seat on the Santa Fe Trail.

CHAPTER XV

The New Order

When General Stephen Watts Kearny and his soldiers arrived in Santa Fe, Demetrio and his friends were highly entertained, from their vantage point on a hill above the Trail itself, by the spectacle of an advancing army. The first contingents arrived at three o'clock in the afternoon, and it was almost six o'clock in the evening before the last of Kearny's forces passed.

The boys were much impressed with the blue uniforms of the American military men. Suddenly, Demetrio yearned to be but one thing, a drummer boy. He looked at those Missouri lads, not too many years older than he and handling their drums in a soldier-like manner, and made up his mind that a drum would have it all over the ancient harpsichord or even the violin. However, the boy remembered that even if he were older, he might not be acceptable to the blue-coated men of Kearny's army. Maybe these hundreds of men who were coming down the Santa Fe Trail might even view him as an enemy. Since Demetrio didn't feel like anyone's enemy, he shrugged his shoulders and followed his playmates. They took a short cut across the river and ran toward the plaza where ceremonies were to be held in the *portal* of the Palace of the Governors.

As the boys neared the Palace, they immediately saw that a red, white and blue banner fluttered overhead, replacing the flag of the Republic of Mexico that had flown from the ancient building for a quarter of a century. The boys could also see that General Kearny and his staff were being welcomed by the Lieutenant Governor of New Mexico, Don Juan Bautista Vigil y Alarid. They knew that their country had fallen to the American military and that Santa Fe was bowing to Kearny's army as readily as had Las Vegas a few days before. In view of this, they were surprised to behold the cordial scene which was being enacted in the *portal* of the Palace of the Governors, the very building where Demetrio had first seen the light of day.

The boys were not the only ones amazed. Santa Fe residents, as a whole, were alive with curiosity. When they finally learned the details of this bloodless revolution, they were aghast. It had been thought that the governor, Don Manuel Armijo, had led a group of dragoons to Apache Canyon, there to engage and halt "the Army of the West." It was known that the governor had been accompanied by Don Diego Archuleta, second in military command and a stormy but sincere Mexican patriot unselfishly devoted to his country. The two men had engaged in a violent quarrel after leaving Santa Fe. Don Diego was all for repelling the invasion. Governor Armijo was against any such plan, claiming that it was useless and futile. The governor was a general, and Don Diego a colonel, so the latter lost the argument and suffered great chagrin in being forced to abandon the cause which was so important a part of his life.

Governor Armijo fled to the south, presumably to Chihuahua, though there were rumors that he got only as far as his ranch in Lemitar. While there were suggestions that he had been bribed, many felt that he did the only sensible thing and that his action prevented needless loss of life on both sides. Don Manuel was not the type to wage a useless battle against overwhelming odds, nor had he any longing to die for his country. The seclusion of his Lemitar *rancho* was his goal, and he felt fortunate in having this place of refuge. If there was a deal, Don Santiago Magoffin was credited with having arranged it between Armijo and the representatives who preceded the arrival of General Kearny. It was well arranged. At least, El Cañoncito de los Apaches was without defense, and "the Army of the West" came through.

Santa Fe people had denied themselves and undergone privation in order to finance the Armijo forces. Now the dragoons, leaderless and worn out, were straggling back to Santa Fe. The saddest figure in the invasion of 1846 was Don Diego Archuleta, a hero and a statesman who could not even return to his family in Santa Fe. His only crime had been his wish to defend his native land against invasion. However, justice finally triumphed and Don Diego Archuleta was eventually able to return to Santa Fe where he took the oath of allegiance to the new government.

Thus it fell to Don Manuel Armijo's deputy, Don Juan Bautista Vigil y Alarid, to turn his government over to a new order, the conquering United States of America. General Kearny told the people of New Mexico that he and his men desired only the welfare of New Mexicans, that their homes and families would remain unmolested and that in the practice of their religion each individual would be free to follow the dictates of his conscience. Only one condition was changed. They were now American citizens.

Lieutenant Governor Vigil y Alarid was probably the only man in Santa Fe who was calm enough to reply. He rose nobly to his duty. He informed General Kearny that while he and his fellow New Mexicans mourned for the lost power of the Mexican Republic, they had no desire for needless trouble and bloodshed. He thanked General Kearny for his many courtesies, paid a generous tribute to the immortal George Washington and promised in the name of everyone in the Department of New Mexico obedience to the laws of the new regime. An opportunist, perhaps, but a gentleman, this Don Juan Bautista Vigil y Alarid. His distinguished bearing and his faultless speech permitted his fellow townsmen to retire with a minimum amount of injury to their pride and enabled them to bow gracefully to the will of the strong; that he had no choice in the matter in no way detracted from the dignity of his surrender.

So was history made. The reaction in Santa Fe was as chaotic as might be expected. Different factions reacted differently as was only natural. The *ricos* perhaps saw that their power was coming to an end. They looked at their crumbling *haciendas* and knew that as "a race set apart," they could not survive much longer. They viewed seriously for the first time the *americanos* and realized that against all that New England energy, they would be lost. The *peones* were confused by the radical statement which informed them that all men were created free and equal. But, at the same time, it sounded good to their ears and seemed to hold possibilities for the future. The traders and trappers, an important faction in the life of Santa Fe, sensed the dawn of a new economic day. They were largely

Americans, with a sprinkling of French Canadians, and they had made the most of the free and easy life of Santa Fe. Now they were going to face a new government, and they knew that some of their dealings would not bear scrutiny.

Only in the gambling halls of the capital city did life go on as usual. The roulette wheels whirled and spun and stopped on red or black numbers without influence from either Mexico City or Washington. Spain might lose her possessions in North America and the Eagle of Mexico be replaced by the Stars and Stripes, but four aces in a card game or a lucky number at the monte table — still paid off. The *hidalgo* or trapper who had wisely or luckily placed his bet could walk out a *rico* in his own right. In fact, in these halls of chance the pace seemed a little faster than ever.

CHAPTER XVI

Demetrio and the U.S.A.

Little Demetrio saw many exciting things on the plaza that day. When he realized that he was both tired and hungry, he decided that it was time to be heading for home. He also wanted to tell Doña Guadalupe all that he had seen and heard.

As he entered the little *casita* in the Analco, he felt a bit guilty because he had been gone all day. He felt even guiltier when he saw that the *curandera* had been called. Rousing herself, his aunt forced her attention to dwell on the many exciting happenings which he was relating. The boy's day had been a full one and, as always, he wanted to share it with Doña Guadalupe, now almost a recluse in her little home. She was glad to get the straight of what had happened in Apache Canyon, or rather, to learn that nothing much had happened at all. At least, there was no fighting, no bloodshed. The *americanos* had simply come rolling through the Apache Pass and had met no opposition. She was no longer interested in the actions of Don Manuel Armijo. Knowing that she could not exist on hatred and bitterness, she had erased Don Manuel from her mind. She did, however, allow herself a little surge of triumph as she realized that she had survived Don Manuel in Santa Fe. Regardless of the future, the era of Armijo had passed into history.

Doña Guadalupe knew that her own days were also numbered. Not even she could ward off the ailments brought on by advancing years, and she was faced again with making plans for little Demetrio. The *curandera* had said only this morning that there was nothing more she could do for Doña Guadalupe's ebbing strength. Herbs brought from the mountains seemed to have no effect, and the Analco practitioner had even suggested that her patient might try the American doctor who had recently come to Santa Fe. The American traders liked him and even some of the old Spanish families had gone to him for medicine and treatments. Doña Guadalupe knew that she could never take so radical a step. She had lived too long to start describing her symptoms to a man, and even if she could bring herself to do it, the old woman knew that she had not long to live. She knew her own condition well. At best, the American physician might prolong her life for a short time. No, she reasoned, she would not desert the *curandera*. When everything failed, she would be ready for her entrance into a better world.

On the night of the invasion of Santa Fe, Doña Guadalupe felt at peace. She might be one of a conquered people but she was not afraid for she had been able to take care of Demetrio's future. When she was gone, the boy would not be alone. Some days before the *vicario* had called on her, and she had presented her plan to him. Once before she had depended upon the Church to provide a refuge for her boy, and it was therefore only natural that she should rely on the Church again. She wanted Demetrio to become a ward of the *vicario* and to become a part of his household. Furthermore, she wanted all this done while she still lived.

The Santa Fe prelate had acceded to the old woman's wishes and agreed to take Demetrio whenever she wished. A member of one of Santa Fe's oldest families, Father Ortiz maintained a spacious and dignified home which was also headquarters for the Church of Santa Fe. It was called by local residents the *convento*, a term which was a holdover from the days of the Franciscan Fathers. It contained a small chapel, and Doña Guadalupe liked to dwell on the fact that her boy would be a part of such inspirational surroundings. Also, he would soon be enrolled by the *vicario* in a school to be opened by Don Juan Rafael Pacheco. The old Tatty school, having been founded and encouraged by Governor Martínez de Lejanza, had been suppressed by Governor Armijo when he returned to power. Until the opening of the Pacheco Academy, there had been no place for schooling in the life of Demetrio. Later, the *vicario* hoped that the boy could be sent to an advanced academy in Durango. He might even have a vocation for the religious life.

Father Ortiz felt that it was a cruel thing to take Demetrio while his great-aunt still lived but the old woman was adamant on the subject and the *vicario* did not argue. Doña Guadalupe knew better than anyone else how much she would miss the boy but she was ready to disregard her own feelings for the future of Demetrio. A proud woman and a domineering one, she had never been selfish, and New Mexico had softened the old aristocrat. She knew that for her own limited needs, Prudencia would suffice. It was better that Demetrio join the establishment of the *vicario* and that he do it soon.

All these thoughts were racing through Doña Guadalupe's active mind as she tried to give her attention to the boy's description of plaza happenings. He withheld from her only one thing, his ambition to be a drummer boy in "the Army of the West." For some reason, he felt that the time was not right for him to reveal this desire.

Demetrio showed signs of being tired, and old Doña Guadalupe looked long and fondly at the boy who had been her life for a decade. "Come, *mi hijito,*" she said, "you must be hungry. Eat some *posole,* my child, and when you have eaten, bring your violin and play for me. You have made me see what is going on in Santa Fe today and I must think about it."

Demetrio hesitated to leave as it seemed that Doña Guadalupe had more to say. She went on, almost in reverie, "You will remember that I, too, have seen many sights in that plaza. I have seen dancing and merry-making and as I watched, I was a girl again in Veracruz. I have listened to eloquent speeches made by *alcaldes* and as I listened, I grew to understand New Mexico better. This has not always been the case and I daresay that I have been at fault. Possibly, I have felt too much that I am a Mexican and of the *gente fina*.

"In the plaza I have also seen trouble and bloodshed, treachery and treason. Much of it is indelibly etched upon my mind. Sometimes, in the darkness of the night, I see again the debauchery and lust which attended the murder of your father, *mi hijo*. I have told you of this many times, and you must remember it always. Do not fail to tell it to your children. Through them, the story will be passed down to future generations. New Mexico must never forget

Don Albino Pérez and the manner in which he died. He gave his life for New Mexico. Today, the Santa Fe plaza has witnessed another milestone. No one knows what the future will bring, for New Mexico and for you. And now I must talk to you about your future, Demetrio. It cannot be postponed much longer. But first you must have something to eat.''

The boy, becoming grave as he sensed the seriousness in Doña Guadalupe's words, looked carefully at his aunt before going into the kitchen. When he returned he got his violin from its place behind the old harpsichord and with a smile said to Doña Guadalupe, ''I haven't told you of the new songs which I heard today in the plaza. I couldn't understand the English words very well but I liked the music. And the melody, it was strong, strong like the *americanos* themselves. One was called 'Long Long Ago' and the other was 'Ol Dan Tucker.' '' He paused and went on shyly, ''I think I can remember how these American songs went. Would you like to hear them?''

The old woman moved in her chair and replied, ''Not tonight, my son. Later, perhaps I will enjoy hearing the new songs. New eras bring new songs, I know, and a whole new era is being ushered into New Mexico today. I try to meet changes, and I have done it many times, but you must not ask me to revise my taste in music. I have loved the old songs too long and tonight especially, I want to hear the songs which have been a part of my life. Play for me *'Las Mañanitas.' ''*

And so Demetrio put from his mind the *yanqui* tunes he had heard and liked and played *"Las Mañanitas."* Stopping for a little while, he searched in his mind for other songs which would please Doña Guadalupe. Picking up his violin again, he drew his bow across the strings and brought from the instrument song after song, ballad after ballad, all dear to Latin people everywhere and particularly descriptive of centuries of life in Spain and Mexico. Finally, *"La Calandria"* came softly from Demetrio's violin, and he saw that Doña Guadalupe was almost asleep, the strains of the song became fainter and fainter.

In a golden cage, hanging on a balcony
A lonely lark, at her imprisonment, wept.

En una jaula de oro, pendiente de un balcón
Una triste calandria lloraba su prisión.

As Demetrio stopped playing he was aware of reverberations which seemed to make the little house in the Analco tremble on its foundations. From the crest of a hill overlooking Santa Fe, a volley of shots resounded as a salute of thirteen guns echoed over the ancient city of the Holy Faith.

It was the Eighteenth Day of August in Eighteen Hundred and Forty Six, and this was now the United States of America.

The author, having published numerous articles and poems relating to New Mexico history, has spent many years in public life, including three years as City Clerk in Gallup, four terms as Chief Clerk of the New Mexico State Senate, nineteen years as Assistant Collector of Internal Revenue and eight years as Director of New Mexico's Income Tax program. He holds a papal honor as Knight of St. Gregory. He and Mrs. McCulloch, a former teacher in the schools of northern New Mexico, have been blessed with four children, three of whom are living in New Mexico and Arizona.

www.ingramcontent.com/pod-product-compliance
Lightning Source LLC
Chambersburg PA
CBHW051817040426
42446CB00007B/722